STUDY POWER

Study Skills to Improve Your Learning and Your Grades

by
William R. Luckie, Ph.D.,
& Wood Smethurst, Ed.D.

BROOK
L I N E
BOOKS

ISBN 1-57129-046-X

Library of Congress Cataloging-In-Publication Data
Luckie, William R.
    Study power: study skills to improve your learning and your
    grades / William R. Luckie & Wood Smethurst.
        p.   cm.
    Includes index.
    ISBN 1-57129-046-X (pbk.)
    1. Study skills--United States.   2. Students--Time management-
    -United States.   3. Test-taking skills--United States.
    I. Smethurst, Wood.   II. Title.
    LB1049.L47   1997
    371.3'028--dc21   97-44338
                                                        CIP

Book design and typography by Erica L. Schultz.

Printed in USA by Bang Printing, Brainerd, MN.
10 9 8 7 6 5 4 3 2 1

Published by
BROOKLINE BOOKS
P.O. Box 1047
Cambridge, Massachusetts 02238
Order toll-free: 1-800-666-BOOK

Contents

PART A: INPUT SKILLS

PART B: PROCESS SKILLS

PART C: OUTPUT SKILLS

*This book is dedicated
to all our students*

INTRODUCTION

A Systematic Approach to Study

This book is about school success and how it happens, and especially how you can *make* it happen. It turns out that school success is not directly related to intelligence, quickness, ambition, or any other such characteristics. Primarily, it comes from the ability and desire to manage your work and your time effectively. The idea that there could be a unified system for managing study time, studying effectively, and doing well in school is a relatively new one. Our approach grew out of the work of Harvard's Bureau of Study Counsel, but it only became a system after we began to work with it at Emory University.

Harvard administrators in the 1940s built on the belief that it makes no sense to kick students out of school for bad grades — that it's better to keep them in school and just help them to improve their grades. They started with the assumption that students had to be smart enough to complete college to get into Harvard in the first place. Therefore, they concluded, there must be some reason *other* than lack of intelligence why some of the students were getting bad grades. This proved to be true.

Bill Perry, a psychologist, was appointed to head the Bureau of Study Counsel, and he worked closely with Harvard and Radcliffe undergraduates who had run into difficulties with academics. The Bureau began to work intensively with each student who had gotten into trouble on whatever it was he or she needed help with — whether it was writing papers or learning to read faster and better. The Bureau also did a lot of counseling for students who had problems with their family, problems with their roommates, or other personal difficulties.

Harvard has been very successful in supporting students. Historically, Harvard has had the highest graduation rate of any American college; one study estimated that 97% of the students who go to Harvard graduate. The next closest figure is about 80%, and most other colleges fall much farther behind. I suspect that Harvard's extraordinary graduation rate is partly a result of this caring approach to academic success — the simple presumption that *of course* you can succeed.

I [Dr. Smethurst] came to Emory University in Atlanta, Georgia in the early 1970s. I served as head of the Emory Reading Center and Catch-up School, and brought the Harvard experience there. Emory did not have a study support program, so I became it. I began working with study skills at that time, trying to help Emory undergraduates and other students in the area to succeed in school. Many students come to Emory to prepare for medical studies. I often worked with pre-meds who had done very well in high school, but who suffered greatly when they encountered some of the more difficult college courses.

In the mid-1970s, I began to offer a 10-session study seminar for freshmen and sophomores on probation. The Dean's office sent letters to all freshmen and sophomores on probation, inviting them to attend. In the seminar, I introduced students to what was rapidly becoming a systematic approach to study. I showed them how to take better notes, how to manage their time, how to read better and faster, how to memorize, and how to prepare for tests. We worked on test taking and test anxiety, on getting papers done and completing project work — all the skills one has to master to be a good student. And lo and behold, the students began to improve.

The first time a student in the seminar got off probation and onto the Dean's List, it seemed like a miracle. Then, the next quarter, four of these students got onto the Dean's List. These leaps became quite common every time the seminar was offered. I came to realize that Harvard's conclusion that intelligence was not a major factor in grades was true at Emory as well. I later learned that it was true everywhere.

The study system Dr. Luckie and I developed is based on the effective use and management of time, because students are essentially managers. Students are managing scarce resources — their time, energy, and effort — in order to produce a product. In this case, their product is completed work, which is customarily measured in terms of instructor recommendations, grades, and diplomas. It all comes down eventually to wise use of time, because that is the main resource a student has. As a rule, the students who do best in school are not the smartest ones, but the ones who are the most effective studiers and managers of time.

Dr. Luckie and I concluded that effective study skills are teachable and relatively easy to learn. Based on that idea, we developed materials and began to offer study skills workshops. The two of us traveled all over the Southeast teaching study skills. We taught study skills at a camp we held in the summer, and we held study skills workshops on the weekends at Emory and elsewhere.

While we were teaching, we gradually developed our ideas into a system, which we call the Study Power system. We found that ways to study and succeed in school can be taught, and taught well, to students at all levels of sophistication, achievement, and intelligence, and from all walks of life — starting as early as 5th or 6th grade, and including college and graduate students. We now work quite successfully with students at Emory Medical School and internal medicine residents at Georgia Baptist Hospital and the Medical College of Georgia. For several years, we also taught an Evening at Emory course for adults who were planning to go back to school. This was one of our most successful and rewarding teaching efforts. Adults in each of these groups learn many of the same skills that we teach fifth-graders, but at a much higher level of demand. The work differs, but the skills don't. Children and medical students alike have to learn effective methods for listening in class, taking notes, doing project work, scheduling their time use, managing a large project over time, and taking tests.

THE STUDY POWER SYSTEM

In improving study skills, it is important to concentrate on maximizing one variable: time. No one has more than 24 hours in a day, yet some students get much more mileage than others out of the same period of time. How do they do it? There are several keys.

The first key is motivation. The Study Power system assumes that students have some desire to get good grades, learn, and succeed in school. No system of study can help students who don't want to learn. Since nearly all students would like to be successful in school, we rarely encounter a student who simply does not care. With younger students, parents can do a great deal to encourage motivation.

The other keys to maximizing study time involve three main functions: *input*, the actions you perform to enter information into your brain; *process*, the acts you execute to process the information once it is in your brain; and *output*, the functions you carry out to retrieve information from your brain. The diagram on page 4 displays the elements of each major function of the model.

Students usually place the greatest emphasis on the output portion of the paradigm. While this is the area of the model in which students are graded, *output functions are not the only ones that determine your grade*. Most students need to put greater effort into the input and process elements of their study system than they do ordinarily.

Input

The *input* functions are the operations most often ignored by students. Yet these are the most important aspects of study, since they are the information-gathering functions. Information is best gathered a little at a time, early and often — and the best place to do this regularly is in the classroom. Since instructors generally cover nearly all the needed information during class, **listening** is a student's primary skill. Good students are usually good listeners.

Note taking is the second skill needed by a successful student. (It is not quite as important as listening because information cannot be noted if it is not heard and understood.) The notes a student takes in class and while reading become the primary sources for study. They must be accurate and reliable.

Class participation is the only element that appears in all three areas of the study system. Since class participation provides the best opportunity to obtain study information, skillful students are totally involved in class activities. Class participation is more than being involved in class discussion; it also includes being attentive, actively listening, and aggressively seeking out the information presented in the classroom. Good students not only attend class; they also become active consumers of the class product, ensuring that they obtain all the information and knowledge available for their time and/or tuition dollars. A good student is a wise consumer.

THE STUDY POWER SYSTEM

INPUT	PROCESS	OUTPUT
Listening ✓	Self-Management	Test Taking ✓
Note Taking ✓	Time Management	Written Reports ✓
Reading ✓	Learning & Memory	Oral Reports
Class Participation	Concentration	Class Participation
	Daily Review	
	Class Participation	
	Test Preparation	

The final skill needed to obtain information for learning is **reading.** Reading is the primary activity that students think of as studying; most students do view reading as a crucial part of learning.

Process

While input functions are the most important study skills, they are only part of the system. Once the information for study is obtained, the material must also be *processed.* Input operations begin the processing functions, but for learning to be sufficient and lasting, additional processing activities are necessary.

Managing your memory is one important processing function. Memory itself is not usually the primary problem for students; the main problem is one of recall. Often students can remember the correct answers after a test. The trick is to recall the information when you want it and in the manner in which the question is posed. Developing this ability requires processing approaches that increase recall. Several recall techniques are essential components of our study system, and will be discussed.

Concentration, another important process skill, is the most difficult component of the study system. However, some concentration is required for all conscious human behavior, and good concentration is essential for all academic efforts. Most students are unable to concentrate on a single idea, concept, or object for much longer than 30 to 90 seconds. Later in the book we provide techniques and exercises to help you maintain concentration for longer periods of time and improve your comprehension.

At the heart of the processing element of our study system is constant, deliberate, **daily review.** Timely review is necessary for processing information effectively. Recall develops through reviewing material often over time. We present varied methods of review that employ visual, auditory, tactile, and kinesthetic modes for optimum learning.

Instead of engaging in daily review, most students focus too heavily on **test preparation;** many study only for tests, and thus are constantly in the process of catching up. In addition, many students study only through cramming, a very ineffective approach. Test preparation should be integrated into periodic review, as an integral part of an overall approach to learning. To perform well on tests, students must master both details and general meanings. The Study Power system provides a series of tools for learning these two types of information.

Class participation is important as a process, just as it is important as input. For a class to have meaning to a student, the student must first intend to listen, take notes, and maintain concentration. The primary processing function of class participation is directed thinking — mentally questioning, summarizing ideas, and putting information into one's own words. The classroom is the most effective place for this process to begin. Our system provides varied approaches to enhancing the processing of information in the classroom.

The last processing function, **managing time,** is a critical part of our study system, but one that is misunderstood or poorly handled by many students. In our discussion of time management, we demonstrate how to develop a time line, how to organize activities using the steps of the academic process, how to construct a weekly calendar of events, and how to maintain a daily schedule of activities. This planning helps assure that needed work is completed before the due date. It also allows students to complete their academic requirements and still have time for social, athletic, and personal activities.

Output

As mentioned earlier, our study system places the greatest emphasis on the input and process functions of structured learning. The acts outlined above — acquiring knowledge, summarizing information, synthesizing ideas, and so on — involve very high-order thinking and learning processes. These skills not only serve students in school, but also foster lifelong goal achievement. Learning is constant in an information age.

Yet while input and process operations are most important, *output* activities are also critical. To know how to perform and still not perform is folly. While performance requires knowledge and understanding, it also requires the ability to act under pressure and complete the task at hand. Payoff for your studying comes not with the input and process stages, but with output. The first two functions are necessary for performance to happen, but it is performance itself that produces what is most desired and admired.

The area of study that students are generally most concerned with is **test taking.** Many students suffer from test anxiety. We will explain how anxiety occurs, how to recognize the symptoms of anxiety, how to prevent anxiety from occurring, and how to cope with it if it does occur. Test anxiety is best avoided by using a thorough, systematic approach to study and test taking. Although most students already possess some skill in test taking due to their exposure to tests over time, this skill can be significantly enhanced. In this book, we present test-taking strategies for various types of test questions, including essay questions, multiple-choice questions, short-answer questions, and true-false questions. We also present a general test-taking strategy with an emphasis on developing priorities while testing, making the best use of the available time, and following correct procedures. Each test should be a learning experience. Our system provides methods for analyzing the results of each test to help students become better test takers. This analysis also allows students to learn content from the test itself.

Typically, your grade is a product of test scores, one or more written reports, class participation, and possibly an oral report. We introduce several methods for **writing papers,** with advice on how to organize a paper, develop the paper over time, and avoid pitfalls in writing.

We also provide advice on giving **oral reports** — from selecting a topic to preparing, practicing, and presenting the report. Although many classes require some type of oral presentation, many students have little or no experience speaking before a group. Developing this output skill helps many students build up self-confidence.

In addition to tests and reports, every grade includes **class participation.** Even instructors who claim to take no interest in student participation are directly and indirectly influenced by the manner in which a student performs in class. Following the strategies for appropriate class participation discussed in this book can significantly enhance a student's classroom performance.

HOW TO USE THIS BOOK

We have written this book for students and for their parents and teachers. It is the outgrowth of many years of teaching students to study more effectively. We have taught a combined total of more that 75 years (which shocks us a little when we think about it). The sum of all our teaching experience is the lesson that *ways to be a good student can be taught, and can be learned by any student willing to work for them.*

This book is for any student who wants to master study skills in order to learn more effectively, get better grades, and enjoy school more. We hope it will be helpful to parents and teachers as well. We want the experience of reading this book to be a lesson in learning for each reader.

First, to get the most out of this book, *you will need a separate notebook in which to take notes, do the exercises, and answer the review questions. Do all your writing in this notebook.* This will allow you to review your notes easily. As you enter your work into the notebook over time, you will notice how much better your answers to the problems become. For example, as you gain proficiency in the Study Power system, you can compare your most recent summaries with the earliest ones in your notebook. This way, you can see the quality improve dramatically over time.

Your next step is to preview the book and consider what you would like to get out of it. Read the Table of Contents, and think about what each chapter is likely to tell you. Then, having read this introduction carefully, turn through each chapter, noting the chapter titles, subheads, graphs, and charts as you go along. Give some thought to which areas cover your own strengths and weaknesses. Bear in mind that the path to wisdom is to build on your strengths and shore up your weaknesses.

Note how the book is organized. The Study Power system is divided into three separate sets of skills: input skills, process skills, and output skills. The model of input-process-output closely matches the ways in which most school and college classes are conducted. This flexible way of analyzing complex systems can help you to better understand any education or production operation.

After you get a general overview, the next step is to read the book, one chapter at a time. Preview each chapter first (look through it quickly to get a sense of what it covers), then read it thoughtfully. Make any notes you need in your notebook. When you get to the end of a chapter, summarize what it told you in five to nine sentences in your notebook, then work through the exercises and do the suggested activities. This will give you a good understanding of the material, and will build your confidence in your ability to apply the concepts and techniques involved in our study system.*

When you finish reading the book, try to summarize the Study Power system in a paragraph in your notebook. Ask yourself which aspect of the system might help you most, and how you might put it into practice in your studies. Explain the Study Power system to one of your friends, teachers, or parents; tell that person what parts of the system you can use most effectively now, what areas you need the most work on, and how you can apply the system in your own schoolwork.

Review this book and your notes on it from time to time. It is amazing to many of our students that this relatively simple system can be adapted to accommodate almost any academic situation. We have repeatedly heard from students that reviewing their Study Power notes helps them to focus on their work. We suggest that you carry out this review every term, or at the beginning of each school year. You will find that each review brings out new elements of the system that you can use in your work, and new ways you can apply them.

One of the greatest study skills of all is persistence — the ability to "hang in there" and complete tasks in an orderly and timely fashion. As you continue to develop and refine your study skills, you will also be building your persistence. Developing this valuable trait will stand you in very good stead throughout your educational career and in your life's work.

---

* A student workbook for *Study Power* will be available in 1998. To order a copy of the *Study Power Workbook,* call 1-800-666-BOOK or (617) 868-0360, or use the order form on page 147 of this book.

Input Skills

The main purpose of attending school is to learn new skills and information. The skills we use to take in new information and ideas in school are known as *input* skills. (Of course, these skills are used outside school, as well.) The first step toward learning effective study habits is to improve your input skills.

The way to maximize the 24 hours of any given day is to make the most of your time in class. After all, you have to be there — you might as well make the class time pay off for you. With good input skills, you can get real mileage out of your in-class time, and that will take a great deal of pressure off your study time. You will still have to study, but your study time will be much more focused.

Students tend to place great emphasis on preparing for tests, writing papers, and performing other output functions. This is understandable, since it appears that these activities have the greatest impact on grades. But while output skills are important, we place even greater emphasis on input skills. You cannot study material that you have not gathered. And the process of gathering information also helps you learn it. The input skills of listening, note taking, reading, and class participation are at the very heart of study. These are the activities that make learning possible, the activities where you *really* make your grades.

CHAPTER 1

Listening

After time management, the most important academic skill is listening. Listening develops a broad base of understanding on which you can build specific and detailed comprehension; it helps you to make sense of the details you learn later. And because it increases your depth of understanding, good listening also saves study time.

Although you should take the best notes you can manage during class, *concentrate on listening.* Most of the input that students receive comes from listening in class, so students who listen well have a marked advantage over students who do not. Keep in mind that the main purpose of in-class listening is to understand and identify the information you will need later. Don't try to memorize in class. Just try to understand what the instructor is talking about and what you're going to be asked about. You are only *gathering* the information; you will *learn* it later.

Unfortunately, listening can sometimes be difficult. One reason for this is that we seldom practice listening in everyday life. All of us want someone to listen to us, but few of us want to be the person who listens. Another reason listening is difficult is that our brains often demand more stimulation than listening provides. As you try to listen to a lecture, your brain may wander off into thoughts that are much more compelling than whatever the instructor is telling you. Usually we fill our brains with the daily activities of living. In a classroom we receive little brain fodder, so our brains become absorbed quite easily with distant, pleasant thoughts, and listening to classroom information is difficult.

THE PREACHER'S METHOD

The key to improving listening is to keep your mind filled up, by making your listening active. To accomplish this, we propose using a technique known as the "Preacher's Method" of listening (later we'll discuss the Preacher's Methods of reading, writing, and speaking). The name of the method has its origin in an old story about a country preacher who was famous for his sermons. People were impressed by his preaching, and they asked what it was that made his sermons so good. He replied, "Well, it's easy. My secret is that I tell 'em what I'm gonna tell 'em, then I tell 'em, then I tell 'em what I told 'em." We think this preacher has hit upon a basic principle of communication. When listening, it is most effective to first *prepare to listen,* then *listen actively,* and then *summarize* what you've heard. If you use this method, you'll come away with pretty good knowledge of what was talked about. This is a very different experience from simply attending class and letting a lecture wash over you.

Preparing to Listen

It is important to be prepared to listen. Before class, preview and skim the relevant text (we'll discuss how to preview and skim in Chapter 3). Try to predict three topics that your instructor is likely to talk about in class. There is usually a class outline, syllabus, or textbook that will help you make predictions. Sometimes you can make a good prediction even without an outline. For instance, if the instructor talked about the first three Crusades in the last class, he or she ought to get to the Fourth Crusade in the next class. If all else fails, ask the instructor what he or she is going to talk about the next day. Try never to arrive in class without having a reasonable idea of what to expect. That way you're always prepared to listen. Preparing to listen before a lecture is the secret to remembering what you've heard. Learning favors the prepared mind. If you've thought about what you're going to hear, your brain will automatically file and categorize these ideas. This categorizing makes listening and learning easier.

Active Listening

In order to be effective, listening must be active — indeed, energetically so. Try to listen critically, to relate what you know to what is being discussed, and to pick out test questions as you listen. It is usually desirable to work with a partner in this, so that you can share what you have both learned. Working together, try to pick out what's going to be on the test. Since any two people will pick up on different information, your partner's slant on the material will probably differ from yours. Having more than one slant on the information makes learning it a more pleasant task. Learning begets learning.

An ordinary class lecture covers 7 to 10 possible test questions. Pay particular attention to definitions, lists, comparisons, and the like. Also pay special attention to the questions that the instructor poses during the lecture. If an instructor asks a question in class, he or she is apt to ask the same question on a test. Perk up your ears and listen for the answer. Additional guidelines for identifying possible test questions are presented in Chapter 2.

Summarizing

Summarizing lecture content is also very important. With practice, you can learn to summarize main facts and ideas both in your mind and on paper. Communications theory suggests that any communication can be adequately summarized in seven (plus or minus two) statements. Always try to summarize the content of a lecture in five to nine sentences. What was said? What did the instructor mean when he or she said it? As soon as you get a chance, discuss what you've learned with others and write down your thoughts. Make sure you have a clear, legible summary of what was talked about, as well as a list of possible test questions.

BECOMING A BETTER LISTENER

As we have emphasized, listening is *the* most fundamental study skill. If you can train yourself to be one of the best listeners in your classes, you will very likely become one of the best students as well.

In each class period, make a conscious effort to listen well. Get into the habit of thinking before each lecture about what the instructor is going to talk about. And after each lecture, while everyone else is heading for the door, sit for a moment and try to mentally summarize what was said, what the instructor meant by it, and what is likely to appear on the test. You'll find that you remember the material much, much better than you usually do.

How do you get motivated to become a better listener? One way is to look around at your classmates. One of our first assignments to students in our study skills seminars is to observe other students who are supposed to be listening. Watching listeners is fascinating, and it shows you how you can become a much better listener than most of your classmates. Notice how many other people *don't* listen — they daydream, read the paper, talk, doodle, etc. The ability to listen gives you a wonderful advantage over others in the class. Also take note of how the most successful students listen.

What does a good listener do? How do students appear when they are actually listening well? The first giveaway is that they clearly watch the instructor (though not necessarily nonstop). Often they will maintain eye contact with the instructor for relatively long periods of time, and you will be able to observe body language that indicates agreement, doubt, or even disagreement as the discourse continues. Good listeners respond nonverbally — and occasionally verbally as well (although students who ask *lots* of questions in class are rarely good listeners). The best listeners seem to "lock in" on an instructor's discussion, and absorb what is said. This process is highly active, and you will be able to observe expressions and body language suggesting intense involvement.

Good listeners come to class prepared to listen. They try to sit reasonably close to the instructor so that they can not only hear the Great One, but also observe his or her facial expressions and other gestures. Few students stop to realize that the instructor needs to see students listening and responding, so that a two-way interaction will take place. As we have said, nearly all of us who teach will respond to an interested student, and genuine interest is the sincerest form of praise for any teacher.

Some good listeners take lots of notes, while others mostly listen. Some like to tape-record lectures, or work in teams with other students and compare notes afterward. We recommend that you work in pairs or threesomes and run a backup tape, but the most important dimensions are involvement and preparation. The best listeners also summarize what they have heard, trying to make sense of it and relate it to what they already know or expect to learn. These students compare notes, look for possible test questions, and prepare study cards to help them memorize the necessary details.

There is one other characteristic that distinguishes the best listeners in a class: the instructor nearly always knows their names.

LISTENING REVIEW QUESTIONS

1. What are the three steps of the Preacher's Method?

2. How do you prepare to listen?

3. What does it mean to listen actively?

4. What are two ways you feel you can improve your use of class time?

LISTENING EXERCISES

1. How well do you feel you presently listen in each of the following areas? In your notebook, grade yourself on a scale of 1 to 10, and briefly explain.

    a. In class

    b. To friends

    c. To family

    d. To television

    e. To radio

    f. To general conversation

2. In which of these areas do you listen best? Why is it easier to listen in these areas?

3. In which area is your listening the poorest? How can you employ your skills in your best area to your poorest area? In what other ways might you improve your listening?

4. When you attend your next class, observe other people. Ask yourself the following questions:

    a. How many students appear to be listening?

    b. Can you tell when someone is listening?

    c. What are students doing when they appear to be listening?

    d. What is the difference between the people you think are listening and those who don't appear to be listening?

    e. Do you feel you can imitate those who appear to be listening?

5. Try doing what the listeners do. In your notebook, list at least three of the listeners' actions that you employed.

    a. Which of these helped you listen better?

    b. Were there any actions you took that seemed to impede your listening?

    c. Based on this exercise, what can you do in the future to improve your listening?

6. Watch a television news program with a friend. Each of you should summarize the program in three to nine sentences in your own notebook.

    a. Share your summaries with each other.

    b. Compile a summary that both of you agree on.

    c. Was your summary improved?

    d. Were you able to restate the ideas of the news program in your own words?

7. Practice summarizing material from movies, from the radio, from the newspaper, from religious services — from whatever sources are available. Summary is an important academic skill.

LISTENING SUMMARY

1. Listening is hearing with the ears and with the brain. It requires effort on the student's part.

2. Treat classroom time as your most important learning time.

3. There is a "Preacher's Method" of learning to listen. A certain preacher uses the following method:

   a. First, he tells the congregation what he is going to tell them.

   b. Second, he tells them.

   c. Third, he tells them what he told them.

4. You can incorporate this listening skill in the classroom.

   a. *Prepare to listen* by looking over the material being lectured on. Guess what the instructor is going to say. Guessing prepares the brain to deal with new information, even if your guess is not correct.

   b. *Listen actively.* Remember that we hear with our ears, but we listen with our brains.

      • Question in your mind what the teacher is saying by asking in your mind the five *w* questions — *who?, what?, when?, where?,* and *why?* — and one *h* question, *how?* This keeps your mind on what the instructor is saying and keeps you preparing for test questions.

      • Relate what you know to what is being discussed for easier recall.

   c. *Summarize.* Whatever the instructor says, rephrase it in your own words. Keep this process going constantly; it helps concentration. At the end of the lecture, try to restate in your own words what you've learned. Identify 5 to 9 ideas you learned from the class.

CHAPTER 2

Note Taking

As we mentioned earlier, listening in class is far more important than taking notes. If you have to choose between understanding what the instructor is saying and getting it written down in your notes, go with understanding the content. After all, you can always write up your notes after class. However, even when you are a very active listener, you will quickly forget the large majority of what you hear in class. For this reason, you must have a record of what you hear.

You won't be able to get every piece of information into your notes, but try to take down the most important ideas. Make sure you know the main idea of the lecture. Most instructors teach from an outline, with the main idea stated in the topic sentence. You can always ask the instructor about the main idea of the lecture. Of course, in addition to the main idea, you need to record numerous supporting ideas. There are usually between 7 and 10 testable questions communicated in any one class; there can be more or fewer than that, but this is a good range to bear in mind.

MAINTAINING YOUR NOTES

Having an accurate, reliable set of notes for each class is critical to effective study. The management of your class notes, reading notes, study cards, and research material is an important factor in making the Study Power system work for you. Since daily review is the best way to improve recall and to prepare for tests, it is necessary to have all these materials organized and in a safe place, where they will not be disturbed.

Your notes need to be out of harm's way. Students often take notes in composition notebooks, sometimes maintaining a separate notebook for each subject or class. If you use composition notebooks, you probably tend to carry them with you wherever you go. It is easy to forget one notebook, to lay it down while you talk to someone and leave it, or to lose it in any number of other ways. Even if you don't lose it, the notebook could get damaged or destroyed. Avoid jeopardizing your most valuable study source; maintain your notes in a secure place, and never carry an entire set of notes for a term with you anywhere.

To maintain your notes properly, it is important to give some thought to the type of paper you use to take notes and the filing system that supports the review of your notes. Loose-leaf pages or legal pads are usually preferable to composition notebooks, because you can easily file notes written on them. Maintain a file for each day of the week for each subject. For recall to be at its best, you need to review each set of notes for 5 consecutive days. After these 5 days, place the set in the appropriate file. Then, every Monday, review all the notes in your Monday files (e.g., the Monday history file, Monday English file, etc.). Every Tuesday, review all the notes in your Tuesday files. Carry out this procedure for each day of the week. Review each set of notes once a week until the end of the term or until you no longer need to know that information in detail. This allows you to maintain a high level of recall for each subject throughout the term. (It is also valuable to review your study cards [see Chapter 3] in the same manner: review all the cards you have learned once a week until the end of the term.)

IDENTIFYING TEST QUESTIONS

For each class session, make sure you write down at least 7 major ideas, definitions, or other details that are likely to become test questions. There are numerous ways to determine what information an instructor is likely to ask about on a test. For instance, the first thing and the last thing an instructor says are usually important. Also, whenever an instructor gets distracted and then comes back to a subject, that subject is almost invariably a main idea.

Instructors typically say more important things in the last part of the class than they do in the first part of the class. Give yourself a pep talk about midway through the class period, because the most facts are introduced in the last 10 minutes. By this time, many students have writer's cramp, their minds are beginning to wander, and they're starting to get ready to leave. But this is the time when you really need to concentrate on taking notes. Instructors tend to do a certain amount of chatting in the beginning of class, gradually easing into a subject. Later, when they realize how much they have to cover, they get more focused, and they finish up strong. As a note taker, you should finish up strong as well.

There are several other important guidelines to remember for identifying test questions:

- Whenever an instructor gives you a list — three ideas, four major types, five degrees, etc. — put it in your notes; a list is very easy for instructors to turn into a multiple-choice or short-answer question.

- Write down any comparisons (e.g., Type A does this while Type B does that); these also make good questions.

- Make a note of any superlatives — "the most," "the best," "the least," "the first," "the last," etc. These make excellent questions, and instructors can rarely resist asking questions such as *Who was the first such-and-such?, Who was the last?, Who was the best?,* or *Who was the most successful?*

- As a rule of thumb, write down everything the instructor displays on an overhead projector or writes on the board — whether or not you think it's important. This will require you to take down some unimportant information, but it will also guarantee that you get some important facts that everyone else probably thinks are unimportant.

- Write down any information that is repeated during a class or mentioned in several classes. If the instructor talks about a certain idea, fact, or person today, tomorrow, *and* next Tuesday, you can be reasonably sure it will appear on the test.

- Make a special note of any idea the teacher gets excited about, spells out for emphasis, or describes with an unusual or distinctive manner or vocal expression.

Another way to identify important information is to develop and answer relevant *who, what, when, where, why,* and *how* questions. On your paper, draw a line down the middle of a page, and write your questions on the left side. (You may want to use several pages, for different subtopics covered in a text or lecture.) While you're listening to the lecture, or soon afterward, write the answer to each question on the right side of the paper. Designate each idea separately, and skip a line to give yourself room to write down needed information. Put a dash (-) by each idea. Then, for any important ideas, change the dash to a plus (+). Then, if you think an idea will be a test item, change the plus to an asterisk (*). A simple example of this note-taking device appears in Figure 2-1 on the next page.

This note-taking technique is particularly useful in history classes. It can also be modified for other subjects, using different types of questions. For instance, if you were studying abnormal psychology, you could make a page for each disorder, with questions about the symptoms, diagnostic criteria, prevalence in the population, treatments, and so on. After you fill in the answers to your questions, you can use these notes to test yourself; fold the paper lengthwise so you can only see the questions, and try to remember the answers.

FIGURE 2-1.
Sample Note-Taking Page.

WRITE QUESTIONS HERE	WRITE CONTENT HERE
Who was Columbus?	— Young man from Genoa, Italy
(Skip a line.)	
What did he hope to prove about the Earth?	— Wanted to prove earth was round
(Skip a line.)	
When did he discover America?	— 1492
(Skip a line.)	
Where did he sail?	— Wanted to sail to India by going west instead of east
(Skip a line.)	
Why did he have trouble getting money for the voyage?	—People thought earth was flat
(Skip a line.)	
Which countries did he go to for money?	— France, England, Spain
(Skip a line.)	
Which king and queen gave him assistance?	— King Ferdinand & Queen Isabella of Spain

COLLABORATING & TAPE RECORDING

The best way to take notes is in partnerships. Working with a partner gives you the chance to talk about the material you hear in class; talking about lesson content greatly enhances recall. The ideal combination is two students taking notes and listening actively, with a tape recorder running in the background.

Taping lectures is difficult, but it can be very helpful, particularly if you have auditory processing difficulties or other learning disabilities, or if you are easily distracted and your mind tends to wander. The great value of taping a lecture is that it's a solid, reliable backup. It lets you relax and really concentrate on listening without being afraid that you'll miss something. In the event that you and your partner don't understand what was said, you can go back to the tape and relisten to a particular passage as often as you like. (Before taping any teacher, however, get his or her permission. Some instructors do not allow audio taping.)

The Pitfalls of Taping

Despite its advantages, taping does present some difficulties. In addition to logistical and electronic difficulties, there is the inconvenience of reviewing a tape; remember that a 50-minute lecture on tape takes another 50 minutes to review. Also, taping may distract the instructor or other students during class.

Other problems occur when students begin to rely on the tape and cease to pay attention during class time. *Don't stop listening and taking notes!* Students taping a lecture often think they do not need to listen in class because they can go over the tape later. This is foolish. Why spend twice as much time on the material? If you listen and take notes in class, you do not need to listen to the entire tape after the class is over. You only need to listen to the parts of the tape that can help answer specific questions you have about your notes.

Another problem is that taping can be misunderstood. Listening to a tape, you miss the body language of the instructor, which often provides more information than the spoken word. The tape also has a flat sound. It does not always reflect the instructor's speech patterns, and often fails to convey the instructor's emotional responses. Moreover, instructors will some-times say things that are incorrect in an effort to create interest or to emphasize a point. The correct information may be displayed on the chalkboard or overhead projector but never spoken, and thus, not recorded.

If you are careful not to fall into these taping traps, taping can be extremely useful. In the main, it's a good idea, and we urge you to try it. But it is *not* an excuse to stop listening and taking notes!

REVIEWING NOTES

The most important benefit of note taking is that it gives you material for immediate review. Review each day's notes that same day or night, and continue to review them periodically during the term, so that the information never gets cold. Review each subject for at least 5 minutes every day. As you review, edit and expand on your notes. There will always be some material that you didn't write down, and there may be some notes that you're already having trouble reading. Within the 2 or 3 hours after a class, while your memory is fresh, make sure your notes are legible.

The *learning curve,* a diagram of how much information people remember in varying situations, is useful in understanding how reviewing notes affects recall. Because it shows how quickly one forgets information in different circumstances, it could also in jest be called the *forgetting curve.* See Figures 2-2 and 2-3 for an illustration of this curve. As the diagram shows, without review, your recall falls off sharply. Unless we review, we recall only 20 to 25% of what we hear 6 days later. Over 6 months, we remember only about 22% of what we hear and 24% of what we see. (Recall is better for our own actions; over 6 months, we remember 94% of what we do and 76% of what we say.)

Brief daily review of notes stops this fall-off of information recall. *Review your notes every day.* No large investment of time is necessary, since you can review an hour's worth of notes in 1 to 2 minutes. If you review your notes for 5 consecutive days, you will be able to recall that information at 80 to 85% accuracy for 6 days. (This recall fades significantly after 6 months.) These percentages demonstrate the importance of taking notes and reviewing them daily. They also emphasize the value of discussing your notes with a partner, since you remember what you say much better than what you hear or read.

In Figure 2-3, note that recall drops each day. With daily review, you can maintain a higher level of recall. After reviewing your notes for 5 days, you should continue to review them once a week until the end of the term or until you no longer need to recall most of the information.

While you're reviewing, you can also organize your notes, draw arrows connecting pieces of information, and make annotations and additions. Write questions and comments to yourself in the margins. Consider using "law-ruled" paper, large yellow pads which have a wide margin (about a fifth of the width of the paper). Alternatively, you can draw a large margin on ordinary paper. Gradually, your notes will take on the characteristics of a journal; they will begin to reflect your thoughts and your questions, and they will become invaluable study aids.

FIGURE 2-2.
The Learning Curve: recall of information read or heard, without review.

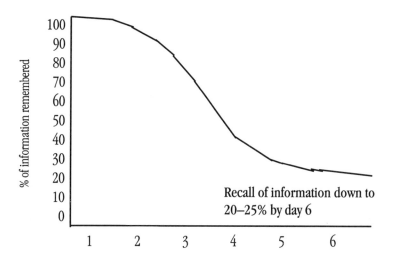

Recall of information down to 20–25% by day 6

FIGURE 2-3.
The Learning Curve with Daily Review.

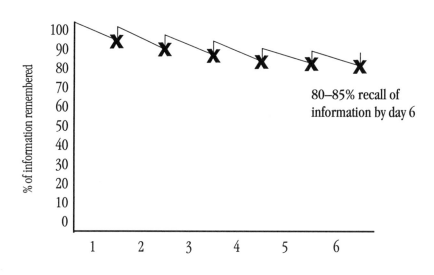

80–85% recall of information by day 6

NOTE TAKING REVIEW QUESTIONS

1. Why do you need a note taking partner?

2. What is the most important time during class to listen and take notes?

3. Name at least two methods you can use to take notes.

4. Why should you try to improve your notes after class?

5. What does it mean to annotate your notes?

6. What minimum number of times should you review your notes?

NOTE TAKING EXERCISES

1. Listen to a radio newscast with a friend.

    a. Prepare to listen.

    b. Prepare to take notes (have paper, a pencil, and a place to write, and prepare the paper for taking notes).

    c. Try to take notes as carefully as possible on at least three news features.

    d. After the newscast, improve your notes the best you can.

    e. Compare your notes with your friend.

2. Evaluate your notes and your friend's notes using the following criteria:

    a. Did each set of notes contain the major ideas expressed in the newscast?

    b. Were the notes spaced so that other information could be added to them?

    c. Was each idea designated in some manner to separate it from other ideas?

3. Follow the instructions in Exercises 1 and 2 to practice taking notes from a class lecture, a TV program, a conversation, and other areas of communication. Again, compare and evaluate your notes against those of a friend.

NOTE TAKING SUMMARY

1. Don't expect to be perfect. No one ever takes down every word from a teacher's lecture, and you shouldn't even try to.

2. Keep your notes in a safe place.

3. Use loose-leaf paper or legal pads instead of composition notebooks.

4. Maintain a file for each weekday for each subject.

5. Try to identify test questions. Pay particular attention during the last 10 minutes of class, and be sure to write down

   a. the first and last things the teacher says;

   b. any idea the teacher repeats;

   c. any list, comparison, or superlative;

   d. any idea that is put on the board or appears on an overhead projector;

   e. any idea the teacher spells out for emphasis;

   f. any idea the teacher gets excited about;

   g. any idea the teacher describes with unusual or distinctive expression; and

   h. any idea the teacher tells you to write down.

6. Develop and answer relevant *who, what, when, where, why,* and *how* questions, using a two-column note-taking device.

7. Go over your notes with a partner to fill in any gaps in information.

8. Use a tape recorder to play back any information that you didn't understand in class or that you want to check on.

9. Summarize each lecture in 5–9 sentences, as soon after the lecture as you can.

10. Add to your notes from memory, your reading, and your partner's notes.

11. Review your notes in every subject for at least 5 minutes every day.

CHAPTER 3

Study Reading

The third major input skill you need to work on — one that pays off handsomely in learning to study more effectively and getting better grades — is study reading. Although students get the most information by listening in class, there is still much information acquired by reading, and particularly by study reading.

There are many different kinds of reading. By *study reading,* we mean reading difficult material in order to (a) develop a broad understanding of the material and (b) identify the *specific* information that you need to learn. There are important differences between understanding and learning, in the sense that we use the terms here. Many students *understand* what an expected test is going to be about. They go over their notes with their friends, they discuss possible test questions with each other, and they generally understand the material — but when they go to class, they may do badly on the test. Too often this is because of what they did *not* do. They may have *understood* the material, but they didn't learn it with the specificity with which they needed to know it. They didn't know the details well enough to answer those hard multiple-choice questions that deal in ambiguity, that typically turn on subtle matters of definition. The hard truth is that *unless you know the important definitions and the specific details cold,* you will not be able to do well on most multiple-choice and short-answer tests.

Just as understanding is confused with learning, many students confuse *study reading* with *studying.* Study reading is not studying — it is *gathering information to study.* You do not consider yourself to be studying when you listen in class and take notes; you realize you are acquiring the material that you will study later. Study reading is the same sort of process. It is actually very similar to listening. When you study read, you should think of yourself as listening to the author of the text, just as you listen to the instructor in class.

THE PREACHER'S METHOD

The purposes of study reading — to identify the information you will have to memorize and to understand the broad picture — are also the two major tasks in listening. The methods for listening effectively and reading effectively are also similar. Think about what the preacher did. The preacher's method for reading more effectively is like his method for listening well: *preview what you're going to read about, read it very actively,* and *summarize it when you finish.*

Previewing

The first step in study reading is to preview, to figure out what it is that you're going to be reading. Read the title, all the subtitles, and any boldfaced text. Read the introduction or the first paragraph. Look at any pictures, charts, graphs, or diagrams, and accompanying captions. Read any questions at the end of the chapter, and read the summary or the last paragraph. Think about what you're going to be reading, and what the main idea is likely to be. Also consider whether you already know something about this subject. The whole process of previewing should take no more than 5 minutes. Still, these short steps will give you a pretty good idea of what the text is going to be about. By a "pretty good idea," we mean 10-20% comprehension of the chapter, and maybe more — depending on what you already know about it to begin with.

Skimming

The preacher's method suggests that after you preview, you should read the material. You'll read it better, however, if you skim it first. Skim quickly; limit yourself to about 30 seconds per page. There are many methods of skimming, including *dynamic skimming, sampling,* the Evelyn Wood speed reading system, and perhaps a hundred or more others. The one we use — "First, First, Last" — is a sampling method of skimming, and it's quite successful with all the groups we teach.

"First, First, Last" skimming proceeds as follows. After you preview the material, read the *first* paragraph carefully, then read the *first sentence* in every paragraph that follows, and then read the *last paragraph*. Since you've already previewed the material, you should begin with about 10 or 20% comprehension. Once you skim, you'll get up to about 50% comprehension. After you've skimmed the text, reread the summary. By this point, you'll really know quite a lot about the material — enough to listen well to a lecture on it, and it takes surprisingly little time. A chapter that takes an hour to read can be previewed and skimmed in only 10 or 15 minutes. This saves you 45 minutes and should leave you with 50% comprehension to build on in the classroom.

After previewing and skimming, you're prepared to listen well in class. Since you know 50% of the information, you know more than most other students in the class. This is enough to make you curious, attentive, and involved. Also, when you know about 50% of what the instructor is talking about, you are able to ask intelligent questions and have a very good grasp when you get through. This sort of active listening will deepen your understanding, and it will help you to identify questions that are likely to appear on tests.

Active Reading, Note Taking, & Study Cards

After class, read the material carefully. Read in 20- to 30-minute segments, and take a break after each segment. It is hard to maximize concentration and stay sharp for much longer than that. Many students who attempt to read an entire text without stopping slip into a trancelike state; they may be looking at the book, but their minds are miles away. To help you avoid this, we recommend a procedure called *chunking:* divide the reading into small, easily digested portions, and focus on finishing one chunk at a time. After you read each chunk, take a few moments to restate its main ideas in your notes and fit it into the context of what you have read so far.

Reading, like listening, should be a very active process. Ask yourself questions and mark or highlight the book. As you have thoughts on the material, write them in the margins or on sticky notes. You may also add to class notes or prepare possible class note outlines prior to attending class.

Read with a pencil, and put together your notes from reading. Transfer these notes, in a summary fashion, to a separate piece of paper. Then create **study cards**, 3 x 5" cards with information on dates, processes, terms, people, formulas, and so on. An example of a study card is given in Figure 3-1. You may want to color-code the cards for different subjects (e.g., green for biology, blue for math, and so on). Use only one term, process, person, etc., per card. Put complementary pieces of information — term/definition; date/event; process/use; person/accomplishments; formula/use; etc. — on opposite sides of the cards. You will use these cards in daily review (see Chapter 8).

FIGURE 3-1.
Example of a study card.

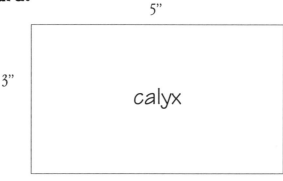

5"

3"

calyx

FRONT OF CARD

5"

A ring of sepals
at the base of a
flower

3"

It's what you have left
after you eat a strawberry.

BACK OF CARD

Summarizing

After you've previewed, skimmed, carefully read, and taken notes on the material, you have 90-plus percent comprehension. And you have completed the first two steps of the Preacher's Method process. The third step — summarizing — is a crucial one. As you read, summarize the material in your mind. Restate the content in your own words. Make the material briefer, more distinct. Make it your own. As you carry out this mental process, you are not only gathering the information, but also processing it into material you can more easily learn. Add your summaries to your class notes. If you review these notes for 5 days just as you would lecture notes, you will retain about 80 to 85% of your reading material.

Summarizing involves asking questions such as *What does it mean?*, *What questions would my instructor ask me on a test about this chapter?*, *What definitions are important; what terms, what identifications, what ideas are important?*, and *What kind of essay would I be asked to write about this topic?* If you can come up with several possible essay questions, you can be reasonably sure that one of them, or some combination of them, will find its way onto the test.

As part of your summary, ask yourself how this material fits with information that you've learned before — in earlier chapters, in earlier class lectures, in other courses, or in other parts of your life. Answering discussion questions makes you develop connections between pieces of information. Often textbooks have good discussion questions at the end of the chapter, and those can really help you. Sometimes they don't, however, and our summary matrix can serve as a substitute.

The *Comprehension Summary Matrix* (see Figure 3-2) is a framework to help you summarize what you read on the basis of answers to the questions *who, what, where, when, why,* and *how.* It also helps you identify the main idea and three or four minor ideas, and it includes space for recording a general summary (five to nine sentences). This method gives you, on one page, a fairly elegant summary of what the material says.

The summary matrix is really effective for literary and informational reading, for history, and for other types of reading with many answers to the questions *who, what, where, when, why,* and *how.* For example, a short story or an account detailing a scientific discovery lends itself to this sort of summary. It's less effective for a chapter on chemistry, and not very effective for math.

There are other techniques that work well for different subjects, following the method of previewing, skimming, reading carefully, and summarizing. For instance, with math, after you preview and skim, you should read with a pencil, working out the examples and problems in the text. That way, you not only understand a topic; you also have practice working through problems in that area. And you have the great advantage of being prepared to talk about the material and listen to the instructor in class. Anyone who has ever failed to understand the topics discussed in a math class will remember how baffling that is. But if you understand what the instructor is talking about, the lecture makes sense; you can follow it, and you feel very much a part of the discussion. Math instructors are often very appreciative of students who understand.

IMPROVING YOUR STUDY READING

How do you learn to read more effectively? Just as playing a lot of tennis will help to make you a better tennis player, doing a lot of reading will help to make you a better reader.

FIGURE 3-2. Comprehension Summary Matrix.

PREVIEW

Who		Main Idea	
What			
When		Minor Idea	
Where			
Why		Minor Idea	
How			

SKIM

Who		Main Idea	
What			
When		Minor Idea	
Where			
Why		Minor Idea	
How			

READ

Who		Main Idea	
What		Minor Idea	
When		Minor Idea	
Where		Minor Idea	
Why		Minor Idea	
How		Minor Idea	
One Sentence Summary			
Concentration Grade	Comments:		

Our standard recommendation is to read at least 30 minutes each day during the school term, and an hour or more each day whenever school is not in session. Find books, newspapers, or magazines that interest you, that you can read relatively easily, and that will bring you real understanding and enjoyment. That should lead you to read more and more — and to read more and more effectively. We tend to read more efficiently when we are interested in what we're reading. Try to read the most interesting materials you can find on a daily basis.

Never lose sight of the principle that reading for pleasure is the key to becoming a better reader. Students who read every day can develop their reading skills enormously. As you begin to read more rapidly and effectively, your reading will begin to have a more profound influence on you. You will develop a better vocabulary, become a better student, and have more time for the things you want to do *besides* studying.

Also try to improve your reading speed, because reading quickly improves comprehension. You need to be reading more rapidly than you can talk. If you don't read quickly, you tend to get bogged down in details.

Remember that you're reading to understand and to identify questions, not to learn the material. Don't try reading to memorize, because that doesn't work very well. Avoid rereading the same paragraph over and over again. Later we'll discuss how to memorize, but it's not by rereading. The best way to read for understanding is to preview, skim, read thoughtfully, mark up the text, and take notes, so that you can come back to it later and memorize it.

Typically, students' time use in study reading is terrible. Students tend to study as ineffectively as they listen, so there's enormous room for improvement — the opening is there for you to take it. If you can study read effectively, you'll have a major edge on your competition.

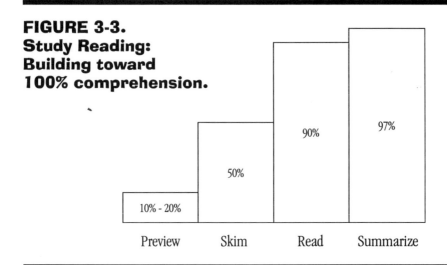

FIGURE 3-3.
Study Reading:
Building toward
100% comprehension.

10% - 20%   50%   90%   97%

Preview   Skim   Read   Summarize

STUDY READING REVIEW QUESTIONS

1. Name two ways to improve your reading comprehension.

2. Why is it so difficult to comprehend material when you're study reading?

3. Why is reading not studying?

4. How do you apply the Preacher's Method to study reading?

5. When you skim after previewing, about what percent of the information should you expect to comprehend?

6. What are the 5 *w*'s and the *h*?

7. How do the 5 *w*'s and the *h* help your reading comprehension?

8. What does it mean to chunk?

9. How does summarizing help you comprehend reading material?

STUDY READING EXERCISES

1. As you read for pleasure, try following the Preacher's Method that we outlined earlier. Practice as you read your newspaper, as follows:

   a. When you're about to read a newspaper story, read the headline.

   b. Before you start to read, think about what the main idea is likely to be.

   c. Read the first paragraph, which should tell you something about who did what, where, when, why, and how.

   d. Then read the rest of the story actively, and summarize what you read in five to nine sentences.

   With practice you'll get better and better at reading quickly and explaining what you've read. You'll surprise yourself by being able to come up with details of what you've read long after you put the paper down.

2. Select a textbook you are now using or one you will use next term. It may be best to select one that you view as difficult.

   a. Preview the next chapter you will be studying or the first chapter you will use next term. Carefully follow these steps:

      1. Look at the title and think about what it tells you.

      2. Read the introduction or the first paragraph of the chapter.

      3. Go through the chapter quickly. Look at all illustrations, pictures, diagrams, graphs, etc., and read the headline captions. Also look at all the boldfaced type.

      4. Read the summary or the last paragraph of the chapter.

      5. Answer the 5 *w*'s and the *h*. Write down the main idea of the chapter and two or three other points you have learned.

   b. Get together with a classmate and share with each other what you saw as the main idea and minor points, as well as your answers to the 5 *w*'s and the *h*.

   c. Make a list of questions that you think should be answered in the text.

   d. Evaluate how much of the information you feel you know and what you think are the main things you still need to learn.

3. Teach a person who has not read this book how to study read.

   a. Tell the person you teach how study reading works, how it differs from reading for pleasure, and how to improve reading comprehension.

   b. Have the person carry out Exercise 1.

   c. Evaluate the process with him or her.

   d. Make sure this person can correctly answer all the review questions for study reading.

STUDY READING SUMMARY

Study reading is very different from what most people think it is. Most people think you just open your book and read from beginning to end. That approach may work with a newspaper, but it doesn't work very well with texts you're going to be tested on. Reading is similar to listening, and the way you study read is similar to the way you listen: prepare to read, read actively, and then think about what you've read. The steps you should be taking are as follows:

1. **Previewing (5 minutes; 10%-20% comprehension)**

   a. Read the title and all subtitles.

   b. Read the introduction or first paragraph.

   c. Read any boldfaced text.

   d. Look at any pictures, charts, graphs, or diagrams, and their captions.

   e. Read any questions at the end of the chapter.

   f. Read the summary or the last paragraph.

   g. Identify the main idea and one or two minor points.

   h. Relate these ideas to what you already know.

2. **Skimming (5-10 minutes; 50% comprehension)**

   a. Read the first paragraph carefully.

   b. Read the first sentence in every following paragraph.

   c. Read the last paragraph.

   d. Reread the summary.

3. **Active Reading (20- to 30-minute segments; 90+% comprehension)**

   a. Chunk the reading into small parts.

   b. Highlight the book or mark it with comments and questions.

   c. Take notes on the reading.

   d. Transfer your notes to a separate piece of paper.

   e. Create 3 x 5" study cards that you will study daily.

4. **Summarizing (90-100% comprehension)**

   a. Briefly summarize the material, in your own words.

   b. Add your summaries to your class notes.

   c. Think about what test questions could be asked on the material.

   d. Relate the material to what you already know.

   e. Answer questions on the material, using textbook questions or the Comprehension Summary Matrix.

CHAPTER 4

Class Participation as Input

Class participation is a part of all three dimensions of the study system. If you attend a tuition-based school, the classroom experience is what you pay for. Schools, at all levels, are organizations designed to house, care for, and support classrooms. Classrooms are where you gain the input (information, skills, attitudes, and values) the school expects you to learn. Good students take advantage of the classroom experience. Since attendance is usually required, you may as well learn all you can from each class.

The first consideration for good class participation is one of intention. For the classroom to be a great source of learning, you must *intend* to learn. You should attend class fully expecting to take in whatever information is provided. You should also come with an intention to cooperate. Cooperation with other class members and with the instructor opens up numerous possibilities for learning. Learn from your classmates. Talk to them about what was said and performed in class. Be involved in class discussion.

Another attitude you should possess is one of aggressiveness about learning. Go to class with the attitude of an intelligent consumer. You pay for the class experience — with tuition or tax dollars — and you should demand in mind and action that it be worth the price. Schooling is a very costly purchase, and must be pursued with the vigor of one who refuses to settle for less than the best. You are also spending a resource of equal or greater value than money — time. Time should be utilized as aggressively as money. Go into each class expecting to understand everything you hear. Expect your instructors to be prepared, not to waste time, to be clear, and to provide adequate explanations. Allow no one, including yourself, to rob you of your chance at learning.

PREPARING FOR CLASS

Appropriate class participation demands that you be prepared to attend class. Too often, students attend class as if they are there to be entertained and they need no prior knowledge to perform well in class.

Before going to class:

1. Look over the part of the textbook that will be discussed during class time.

2. While looking over the text, identify and familiarize yourself with any new vocabulary. The most important input you need to receive from class is an understanding of the content. If you are not familiar with the vocabulary, it will be extremely hard to understand what the instructor is covering.

3. Develop questions about the material to be covered in class. Learning is much more likely to occur if you go to class with questions you want answered than if you have no idea what you wish to know. A student who poses questions in her mind about an upcoming class is better prepared than one who has read the entire chapter.

4. A final way to prepare for class attendance is to think about the subject matter for a short time prior to class. Consider what you already know about the subject or related subjects. Ask yourself the five *w* questions and the *h* question: *who, what, where, when, why,* and *how.* These questions help guide your thought processes and prepare you to participate effectively in class.

CARDINAL RULES FOR INPUT

1. Remember the Preacher's Method:

    a. Tell 'em what you are going to tell 'em.

    b. Tell 'em.

    c. Tell 'em what you told 'em.

2. The best learning time is class time.

3. If you want to learn something, talk about it.

4. Listen, read, summarize, and write down your summaries.

5. A mental summary is saying material to yourself in your own words.

6. Learning is easy. Listening is hard.

7. Intention is the first act of performance. *Intend* to listen.

8. When listening, fill up your mind with what is being said.

9. Good students are good listeners.

10. Reading is listening to what the author has to say.

11. Keep a record of how well you listen and read.

12. Reading speed matters. Read quickly.

13. Reading is not studying. It is gathering information to study.

14. Read in chunks.

15. You need a reliable and accurate set of notes.

16. Your grade depends on class participation.

17. Learning favors the prepared mind.

18. Learning begets learning.

PART B

Process Skills

For everything you do, there is corresponding activity in your brain. Your brain is constantly processing information that you encounter, building information into structures and associations. It files all you see, hear, say, do, or receive in any other way into these knowledge structures; associations within these structures help you recall what you need to know.

By supporting this mental processing, you can make structured learning much less difficult. The process skills involved in study effectiveness include:

- **self-management,**

- **time management,**

- **concentration,**

- **managing your learning,**

- **managing your memory,**

- **class participation,** and

- **preparing for tests.**

We will discuss each of these in the pages that follow. Almost no one is perfect in all of these skills, and most students can profit from instruction in these areas.

CHAPTER 5

Managing Yourself

As we conduct our daily activities, we all manage ourselves with varying degrees of success. Management is not difficult or mysterious, and it is not accomplished only by business executives. Understanding what you do as you manage yourself can help you improve your management skills. Figure 5-1 on the next page presents a diagram of the self-management process.

Management involves making decisions about our *direction* (where we want to go or what we want to do), our *plan* (how we will get somewhere or do something), our *implementation* (the acting out of the plan), and our *evaluation* (judgments about how well we have performed or if the activity was worthwhile).

Consider the following example. Suppose you wanted to go to the store. Deciding to go to the store establishes a direction. You must then plan how you will get there; you should decide what route you will follow, and whether you will walk, drive a car, ride a bicycle, or take a bus. Next, you must implement the plan, making any necessary decisions along the way. For instance, you may follow an alternate route because of a traffic jam or other obstacles. As you complete the trip to the store, you decide if the trip was satisfactory, and you evaluate your actions. (In reality, you make most of these decisions simultaneously, and you may replan or redirect as you evaluate and implement your actions. However, you do constantly make decisions about all four areas.)

Pay attention to the roles these four decision areas play in your daily actions. By

FIGURE 5-1.
The Management Process.

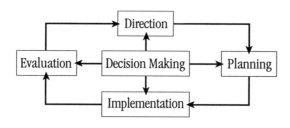

being more aware of your decisions and actions, you can improve your ability to manage yourself.

PRINCIPLES OF DECISION MAKING

Each decision we make has risks associated with it. Because of these risks, making decisions is often very difficult. As you make decisions, keep in mind four basic principles:

1. Never risk more than you can afford to give.

2. Never risk more than you have.

3. Never risk more than you can get in return.

4. Follow your intuition.

The first principle refers not only to financial ventures, but to all decisions. Never take any risk that demands more of yourself or your resources than you are willing and able to give. You alone know what you can afford — in terms of time, energy, emotions, and so on.

The second principle implies that you are limited in resources. You do not have an unlimited supply of energy, time, space, or money, and you cannot risk more of these resources than you possess. Any decision uses one or more of these resources, but no action should deplete all your resources in any given area.

The third principle suggests that you view each decision in terms of what it will produce for you. Take a risk only when you can expect to profit from it. This may appear to be a selfish principle, but even unselfish risks should give you a feeling of satisfaction — which in itself can be a very high return on your investment. Again, only you know what kind of return will make a risk worthwhile.

The last principle simply asserts that you should feel good about your decision. No one can make your decisions for you. You may feel that your parents or friends have forced you to decide or act in a certain way, but this is almost never true. When you allow another person to decide for you, you are still making a decision — the decision to make the choices that another person wants you to make. While this type of decision is not necessarily bad, you should be aware that you *are* making a choice; determine how you feel about that choice and its consequences.

A decision is a commitment — one you are willing to trust and to abide by. All decisions commit you in some way. For instance, when you choose one person as a mate, you commit yourself to that person and eliminate all others from consideration. If you choose to go to college, you may be eliminating the possibilities of traveling, of beginning to earn money, and of many other options at your disposal. You are also committing yourself to studying and going to class; neglecting to study or attend class violates your decision to go to college.

Keep in mind that many decisions limit your choices for the future, but some actually expand your options. It is important to choose those alternatives that open up more possibilities for future choices. The decision to go to college is an example of one that provides you with great opportunities for future decisions.

ESTABLISHING YOUR GOALS AND OBJECTIVES

A goal is a direction you want to follow or an end result you want to attain. Goals cannot be attained immediately; they provide direction for decisions until they are achieved. Setting goals requires long-range plans, and attaining goals requires long-range activities. If you elect to go to college, your plan should include at least the following elements:

a. how you will select a college;

b. what you wish to study;

c. how you will finance your college education;

d. where you will live;

e. what courses you will take, and in what order; and

f. what type of social life you will desire in college.

The components of the plan are shorter-range objectives that are essential to accomplishing your goal. Each component of the plan will include several subcomponents — objectives that are more specific and shorter in range, and that direct your immediate actions. For instance, one objective in your long-range plan deals with the courses you will take in college. An appropriate shorter-range objective would be to complete the required English courses within 2 years. This is a much more definite statement, and it identifies the expected accomplishment within a specific time frame. Getting an A in your first-term English course is an even more specific objective; it specifies not only a relevant time frame, but also a desired level of achievement. The final step is breaking each course goal down into the specific products you will be graded on. Figure out what actions by you, and by *when*, it will take to get an A on each component of each course.

These shorter-range objectives require you to develop written plans. While your long-range plans should be clearly defined in your mind, you may not necessarily write them down. Plans for meeting specific objectives, however, should direct the details of your daily actions; therefore, they are best recorded and closely followed. If you write down what you need to do to accomplish each goal, and then set a time and a place to get it done, you will find that your time begins to take care of itself.

MANAGING YOUR ACADEMIC ENVIRONMENT

To accomplish your academic goals, it is essential to develop detailed methods for managing four major areas in the academic setting: your expectations and effort, your study space, your study materials, and your time.

Expectations and Effort

The most important resource you possess is your own determination. In order to get straight A's, you must expect to get A's. Your expectations must be accompanied by effort, the energy you expend to accomplish your goals and objectives. Moreover, you must *hustle* — you must put forth more effort than is required, before it is due.

Hustle — exceeding what is expected or required — is the essential ingredient required for success in our society. The only way an employee can receive a pay increase or move up the organizational ladder is by exceeding the requirements of his or her present position. Success in the academic setting works the same way; to get an A, you must exceed the minimum requirements for an A.

Exerting even a little more effort than is required will bring high dividends. The payoff for hustle exceeds the rewards for a great deal of any previous efforts just to meet the minimum requirements. Hustle is magic — it brings outstanding accomplishment.

Study Space

Finding a good place to study is very important. An appropriate place for study allows you to concentrate more effectively and learn more easily. You probably should not study at your desk; students' desks are often very cluttered. The last thing you want is to have pictures of friends, souvenirs, pennants, and other distracting items. Set up a study space that really works for you, with as few visual and auditory distractions as possible; an empty card table facing a blank wall is ideal.

You need to be comfortable, but not too comfortable. Get yourself a chair that's not too hard and not too soft; a deluxe recliner is inappropriate. Find a chair in which you can be reasonably comfortable, and in which you can work undisturbed by pain or discomfort for 20 to 30 minutes at a time. Nothing should be on top of the desk except a light, a book or notes, something to write with, and something to write on. Keep a clock in sight so that you can keep track of the time; it helps to have one with a second hand, for reasons we'll discuss in Chapter 7.

Materials for Study

A good worker maintains excellent tools for study. The following materials should be readily available at all times:

1. *Textbooks.* After your notes, textbooks are your major sources of study information. Obtain your own copy of the text or texts for each course you take. Consider buying used textbooks; they are less expensive, and they may contain helpful notes from previous owners.

2. *Paper products.* You should keep several types of paper products available, including index cards (both 3 x 5" and 5 x 8"), loose-leaf notebook paper, manila folders, spiral notebooks, and any paper needed for particular purposes (e.g., graph paper for math, construction paper for art, etc.).

3. *File cabinet or file drawer.* Files are very useful for storing notes and research papers in an orderly fashion. They also help in keeping up with study sources, which are often loose materials subject to being misplaced unless stored properly. Maintain a separate file for each course, and keep all study material organized and filed appropriately for ease of access. A file cabinet is most useful for caring for and reviewing your notes, as we recommended on page 17.

4. *Pens and pencils.* A good supply of writing utensils is always needed. Often colored pens

or pencils are necessary for certain classes or a particular type of work. Some students find it useful to color code or highlight material.

5. *Reference materials.* A set of good encyclopedias and a good college dictionary are essential to have on hand. Often, other reference sources — such as a thesaurus, a book of quotes, journals, and other reference dictionaries — are also helpful. Your major sources of reference materials will be the library and the Internet. Try to develop a good relationship with the resource librarian. Become familiar with the reference coding system the library uses and with the layout of the areas you will use the most. Many libraries offer computer search services for a nominal charge, and many Web access systems include search capabilities. These services can save you a great deal of time in locating and previewing reference materials.

6. *Desks and lighting.* A desk that is free of clutter and available for study is an excellent study tool. Make sure you have adequate lighting for study purposes. If you do not already have one, consider purchasing a desk lamp. Very inexpensive models are available, and a good lamp will prove to be a very good investment.

7. *Computer.* Besides paper and pencils, a personal computer is the primary tool you can possess. Information processing skills are essential in today's high schools and colleges. It is important to learn keyboard skills so that you can use computers as word processors for writing papers and reports.

   Computers also give you access to the Internet. The World Wide Web is a major source of information and can serve as an excellent tool for researching papers and reports. And since almost every college or university now provides E-mail access to its faculty and students, many professors and departments E-mail information directly to students about opportunities, schedules, appointments, and even assignments.

   Many colleges now require students to own a specific type of computer with certain kinds of software. If you know what college you plan to attend, find out if there are any computer requirements there; if there are, become familiar with the appropriate computer and software as soon as possible. If you plan to buy a computer, it is better to purchase one with more power than you think you need, because in time, greater and greater demands will be placed on it.

Time Use

It is to any student's advantage to have a time-use plan. Try to follow our cardinal rule of time use: *Study every subject a little bit every day.* Each day — including Sunday and your birthday! — set aside *prime study time*, an hour to two hours of concentrated study. It can be split into several shorter sessions if necessary, but the time commitment of one to two hours is a constant. Prime study time has four major components:

1. First, review your notes from the day's classes, or from the most recent classes you had. Spend about 5 to 10 minutes with your notes from each class. For each class, try to identify questions you expect the instructor to ask on the next test.

2. Second, prepare to listen in the following day's classes. From your notes or the class outline, you should be able to tell what those classes will cover. Preview and skim any relevant texts to prepare for listening in each class.

3. Third, make study cards for the details and definitions covered in your notes, in your classes, and in your reading. Make a plan for learning them.

4. Fourth, review your back notes. If you do this on a daily basis, you're always prepared, and you never get behind.

Pick the best times to study each day, taking into account your schedule and your cycle of alertness. Some people are morning people, some are afternoon people, and many are evening people. Plan to study at whatever time you work best. Be sure to arrange an appropriate study space with all necessary study materials, as described in the previous two sections.

If you keep up with prime study time, regardless of what is happening in school, it will get to be a habit; you will come to depend on it. At first, the schedule may be a little difficult to adjust to. Most students are used to — and indeed addicted to — going through peaks and valleys in their studies, bouncing from crisis to crisis. They'll study Subject A and leave Subjects B, C, and D aside. Then, after the test for A, they'll need to study B and C. And since they've left out D, they'll need to go back and catch up on that. If you work every day for at least a little while on every subject, you avoid this cycle and never get behind. School becomes much more fun!

After your prime study time, go ahead and study for an upcoming test, work on a paper that's due the next week, or deal with whatever daily project is pressing on you. But *never* let go of prime study time. If you do this faithfully, tests will become easier to study for. Papers will get started earlier, since you won't have time for last-minute late-night paper marathons. You'll do better work, and get more sleep as well. You will also have time for other social and physical activities.

SELF-MANAGEMENT REVIEW QUESTIONS

1. When you manage yourself, what do you make decisions about?

2. What are the four guidelines for taking risks? Do you know any other problems to avoid when taking risks?

3. Can you explain why we must all take risks? If you do not think it is necessary to take risks, explain your view.

4. Why is a decision a commitment? Explain the difference between a committed decision and what we often think of as a decision.

5. What is the difference between a long-range goal and a short-range objective? Explain each.

6. Why is a plan so important for a long-range goal?

7. What four major areas of the academic environment do you need to manage?

8. Which of these areas causes you the greatest difficulty?

9. What do you think you can do to improve in that area?

SELF-MANAGEMENT EXERCISES

1. Design a plan for meeting a goal.

    a. Select a long-range goal. (It is best, but not necessary, to select a goal that you really wish to attain.) The goal should be one that would require at least one year — as well as money, effort, space, and time — for you to accomplish.

    b. Determine several short-range objectives you need to complete for your goal to be met.

    c. Arrange these objectives in order of accomplishment (which ones should be completed first, second, etc.).

    d. Plan what you would do during the first month in working to meet your goal.

    e. Determine what you would need to accomplish each week to meet the monthly objective.

    f. Determine what you would do each day of the first week of the first month.

2. Explain why a goal is only a dream if you do nothing about it.

3. Give three reasons why decisions are commitments.

SELF-MANAGEMENT SUMMARY

1. **Areas of Self-Management.** Self-management requires constant decision making. We make decisions about four main areas:

   a. *direction* – where to go or what to do;

   b. *plan* – how to get somewhere or do something;

   c. *implementation* – the acting out of the plan; and

   d. *evaluation* – judgments about one's performance or about whether the activity was worthwhile.

2. **Decision Making.** Each decision we make has risks associated with it. As you make decisions, keep in mind four basic principles:

   a. Never risk more than you can afford to give.

   b. Never risk more than you have.

   c. Never risk more than you can get in return.

   d. Follow your intuition.

   Keep in mind that many decisions limit your choices for the future, while some expand your options.

3. **Goals and Objectives.** Self-management requires you to set goals and objectives at several levels, as follows:

   a. *Large-scale goals* – directions you want to follow or end results you want to attain. Setting goals requires long-range plans.

   b. *Short-range objectives* – components of a long-range plan. These may relate to a term, a year, or a semester.

   c. *Specific, daily objectives* – plans for accomplishing specific items you will be graded on. These objectives should guide your daily actions.

4. **Elements of the Academic Environment.** Students must manage four major areas in the academic setting, as described below.

   a. *Expectations and effort.* You must expect to get A's, exert effort to accomplish your goals and objectives, and hustle (put forth more effort than is required, before it is due).

   b. *Study space.* Find an appropriate place to study, with few visual and auditory distractions. It should be comfortable, but not too comfortable. In addition to a chair and a desk, all you need is a light, a book or notes, something to write with, something to write on, and a clock.

   3. *Materials for study.* Make sure you have all needed materials, including textbooks, paper products, a file cabinet or file drawer, pens and pencils, and reference materials.

   4. *Time use.* Develop a time-use plan. Each day, set aside an hour or two of *prime study time* to review your notes from your most recent classes, prepare to listen in the following day's classes, make study cards for details and definitions, and review your back notes.

CHAPTER 6

Managing Your Time

Henry David Thoreau said, "If you love life, then you must love time, for that's the stuff life's made of." Time management is the key to successful study management. The essential problem is making the most of down time so that time is available not only for study, but for social, athletic, and work events as well.

Your first priority must be class, and your second priority — study — is nearly as important. As a student, you must view school or college as your job. If at all possible, use the hours from 8:00 AM to 5:00 PM as classroom and study time.

For you to manage your time well, you should know how to develop and use a time line, how to prepare and use weekly and daily calendars, and how to use calendars as checklists.

THE TIME LINE

The purpose of the time line is to help you divide up your work over the weeks of a quarter or semester, so you never have too much to do in any one week. Too often students push the work of the term to the very last moment. If you have too much to do at any one time, you *cannot* manage yourself or your time effectively. Often, several major requirements will be crowded into the same time period. The time line allows you to recognize periods when your time will be scarce, and to compensate by spreading your work out over the weeks of the term.

There are several steps in preparing a time line. The first is to obtain a schedule of when each class meets. This schedule should include laboratory sessions, field trips, and any other required or voluntary sessions for each of your classes. A major consideration in managing your time is to assure that you are not overloaded. Most college students should enroll for no more than 15 or 16 quarter or semester hours per term. If you have doubts about your course load, make it smaller rather than larger.

The important factor in college is not how long it takes you to graduate, but whether or not you get A's. Medical schools, law schools, graduate programs of all sorts, and even employers concern themselves not with the length of time you are in college, but with your grade point average. *You should never take a number of courses that will give you inadequate time to get straight A's.*

Once you have lists of the required and voluntary class meetings, you should obtain a list of assignments for each class. Usually, the instructor will give you the course assignments during the first class meeting. You should obtain course requirements by the end of the first week, at the latest. When you have a full list of meetings and assignments, you are ready to construct a time line.

Assume, for illustrative purposes, that you are a first-quarter college freshman with the following class schedule:

Physical Education	8:00 AM	M, W, F	1 credit hour
English 101	9:00 AM	M-F	5 credit hours
Biology 100	11:00 AM	M-F	5 credit hours
History 101	2:00 PM	M-F	5 credit hours
Biology Lab	4:00 PM	Tu, Th	4 credit hours

Assume that History 101 requires the following assignments:

- *Outside Readings:* You must submit a summary of 50 pages of outside reading from the class reading list each Friday for the first 10 weeks of the quarter. Each assignment must be recorded on a 5 x 8" index card. A correct bibliographic entry must be placed at the top of the card. These summaries will comprise 10% of your quarter's grade.

- *Term Paper:* You must write a term paper of at least 15 typed pages, but no more than 25 typed pages. The topic for your term paper is to be chosen from a list of topics provided by the instructor. The term paper shall have a minimum of 15 references, and you should follow the *MLA Handbook for Writers of Research Papers* or the *Publication Manual of the American Psychological Association* in your footnoting, bibliography, and writing style. The term paper will be worth 20% of your quarter's grade. It will be due the Friday of the 9th week of the quarter.

- *Oral Presentation:* You will make an oral presentation to the class of no less than 10 minutes and no more than 15 minutes. Your oral presentation is to be on a topic from the topic list, but shall not be on the same topic you choose for your term paper. The oral presentations will be given two each day, beginning with Monday of the 6th week. You will be called upon randomly to make your presentation. The oral presentation will make up 15% of the quarter's grade.

- *Tests:* You will have a test every 3 weeks — on the Fridays of the 3rd, 6th, 9th, and final weeks of the quarter. The final exam will comprise 30% of your grade. The midterm exam, on the Friday of the 6th week, will count 15%, and the other two tests will count 5% each.

With this information, you are ready to make a time line for the quarter's work. The time line should include the assignments from all courses. (This example uses only the assignments in History 101.) A time line is a method for recording all requirements for your courses in relationship to the time available. The line may be made for any length of time. Since there are 12 weeks in a quarter, this time line reflects 12 weeks of time, as shown in Figure 6-1.

The horizontal line represents time in weeks. The vertical lines represent the Fridays of each week; therefore, the distance from the first vertical line to second vertical line represents the time from Friday of week 1 to Friday of week 2.

Place your requirements for each course on the time line, according to what assignments are due each week. The requirements in history would be recorded as shown in Figure 6-2. A history reading is required every Friday for the first 10 weeks of the quarter, and is so entered. The oral presentation must be ready by Monday of the 6th week; therefore, it is entered as being completed by Friday of the 5th week. The term paper is shown as being due

FIGURE 6-1.
Time Line (12-week quarter).

1	2	3	4	5	6	7	8	9	10	11	12

FIGURE 6-2.
Time Line, Stage 2 (with assignments recorded).

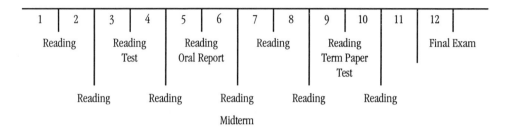

on Friday of the 9th week. The tests are shown on the 3rd, 6th, 9th, and 12th weeks. All assignments for history are now entered on the time line. You should also enter on this same line the requirements and completion dates for each of your other courses.

It may appear that the time line has been completed for the history example. However, it now seems to indicate that you can complete the term paper or the oral presentation in only one week. Of course, you cannot; therefore, you must divide these two tasks into parts that can be completed in reasonable amounts of time. To make these divisions, use the steps of the academic process.

THE ACADEMIC PROCESS

The academic process can be used for any long-term academic endeavor — from a term paper or dissertation to an oral presentation or laboratory assignment. The steps of the process are practically the same in all instances:

- selecting a topic,

- gathering information,

- organizing the information,

- developing an outline,

- preparing the final draft or presentation,

- editing or correcting, and

- preparing the final report.

The following paragraphs describe each of these steps in detail.

Selecting a Topic

Selecting a narrow topic is the most important step in the process. Most students select a topic that is too broad and cannot be covered sufficiently within the allotted time. In fact, most students select a topic on which books could be written, rather than one appropriate for a term paper, research report, or oral presentation. Particularly in college, you are expected to exhaust all available resources on your topic. You should at least cover the major books and periodicals on the subject. If the topic is too broad, the task is nearly impossible. Often the topics suggested by instructors are entirely too broad; however, they will usually allow you to narrow these topics if you seek their permission.

Suppose that as you review the list of topics for History 101, you find three that are interesting to you: the Queen of the Nile, the Hanging Gardens of Babylon, and Alexander the Great.

Your next step is to determine whether there is sufficient reference material available to pursue any of the topics. After searching the library card catalogue, you find there are more than 100 references on Cleopatra, more than 45 references on the Hanging Gardens of Babylon, and more than 300 references on Alexander the Great. As you were looking through the material on Alexander, you found several references on his relationship with his father, Phillip of Macedonia. As you scan the material, you find this to be an interesting topic, one you may wish to report on to the class. This topic — the relationship of Alexander the Great and Phillip of Macedonia — is sufficiently narrow to cover in a 15-minute oral report. You check with your instructor and receive approval to use this topic for your oral presentation.

Gathering Information

The second step in the academic process is gathering information. For a laboratory report or similar research activity, this step involves obtaining data in a laboratory or through a scheduled observation. For most other written and oral reports, this step involves library and computer research. The example that follows focuses on the latter sources of information.

The first step in gathering information is to determine what books and periodicals are available on the topic you have selected. A search of the card catalogue and the *Readers Guide to Periodical Literature* should provide you with this information. Most high school, college, and university libraries also have computer searches available to students, and most Internet access programs have search capacities. The cost of these searches is nominal, and they will save you a great deal of time. Moreover, with a computer search you can be reasonably certain that you have identified all available sources on your topic.

After you have identified all available sources, read the material and summarize (in your own words) any ideas you wish to use. Any material you copy directly should be recorded in quotation marks. Identify each idea by page number, and make a bibliographic entry for each reference source you use. Organize the references with the author's last name first, then list them in alphabetical order and number them. This way, you can refer to any reference by number, instead of with a full citation.

Organizing the Information

After you have obtained the information you need, you can organize the material in one of two ways. One method involves recording each idea on a 5 x 8" index card, with a bibliographic entry — listing the source (or source number) and page number — at the top. In the other method, you record your summaries on loose-leaf paper, making a bibliographic entry for each idea, and leaving a couple of lines between ideas. With either procedure, it is very important to keep track of your bibliographical information.

If you have used index cards, arrange the cards in the order in which the ideas are to appear in the report. If you recorded the ideas on loose-leaf paper, cut the summaries into separate slips. Then paste or tape the ideas on another sheet of paper in the order in which they are to appear. When this task has been completed, an organized "first look" at the report has been prepared.

Developing an Outline

A detailed outline will help you further organize the work. Most students who submit poor papers do so not because they have little to say or because they have not researched the material, but because their work is poorly organized. You can begin to develop an outline as soon as you have selected a topic, and certainly by the time you have begun gathering information. The beginnings of your outline will help you to determine how the material should be organized. The outline cannot be completed, however, until the information is fully organized. The type of outline to be developed will usually be determined by your instructor. If no mention is made of an outline, develop the kind you find to be most comfortable and useful for you.

Preparing the Final Draft or Presentation

Do not begin to write your paper until you have developed a clear, concise, and well-organized outline. Chapter 14 deals with the details of academic writing. For an oral report, practice directly from the outline. Because an oral report should not be read word for word, it is best not to write it out, unless your instructor requires you to do so.

Editing or Correcting

No paper or oral report is ever prepared without errors. Have another person edit your written report or correct your oral report by listening to a practice presentation.

Preparing the Final Report

Write a final draft or complete a final practice.

Use the steps of the academic process to divide up your requirements on the time line. A

FIGURE 6-3.
Estimated time requirements for the steps of the academic process.

Oral Report	STEPS	Term Paper
3 hours	Select a topic	3 hours
8 hours	Gather information	12 hours
2 hours	Organize the information	2 hours
3 hours	Develop an outline	2 hours
5 hours	Prepare the final draft or presentation	12 hours
1 hour	Edit or correct	2 hours
1 hour	Prepare the final report	2 hours
23 hours	TOTAL	35 hours

---

reasonable estimate of the time required for each step is given in Figure 6-3. Note that a term paper usually requires a longer period of preparation than an oral report.

When placing the steps on the time line, begin with the last step in the process and work toward the beginning. Otherwise, all the steps may not be worked into the schedule by the time the final product is to be completed. In our example, prior to including the steps of the academic process, our time line looks like the one in Figure 6-4.

To continue with developing the time line, record the final steps of the process, as shown in Figure 6-5. The last two stages of the oral report (correcting and final practice) and of the term paper (editing and final draft) can be accomplished in just 2 to 4 hours; therefore, in each case, both steps are scheduled to be completed in just one week.

Finally, enter the remaining steps of the process. The time line will appear as shown in Figure 6-6.

FIGURE 6-4.
Time Line, Stage 3.

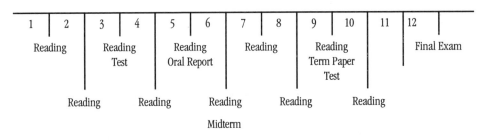

FIGURE 6-5.
Time Line, Stage 4.

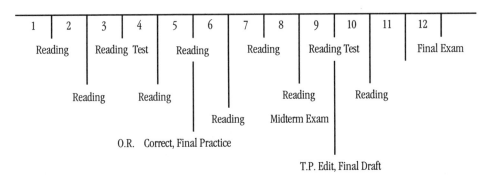

FIGURE 6-6.
Time Line, completed.

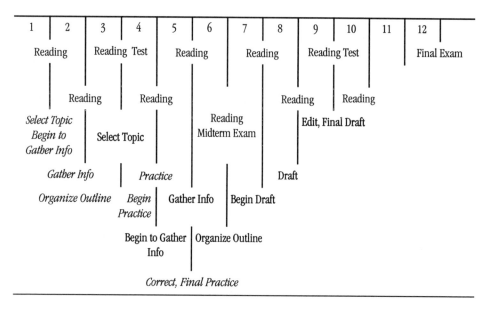

Oral Report: Italics
Term Paper: Bold

Be sure to provide sufficient time for each of the academic steps. For instance, in this example, gathering information and drafting the term paper were both provided 2 weeks to accomplish, since both steps require 12 hours for completion.

After recording all your history requirements, add the requirements for the remainder of your courses. When you have a complete time line for the semester, you are ready to prepare a calendar.

THE WEEKLY CALENDAR

The basic value of the time line is that it organizes your requirements so you can enter them on a weekly calendar. You need a calendar that provides space for every day of the week, including Saturday and Sunday. Such calendars usually devote a page to each weekday, and place Saturday and Sunday together on one page, as shown in Figure 6-7. Typically, hours of the day are specified for each weekday, but not for the weekend days.

FIGURE 6-7.
Sample pages of a weekly calendar.

TUESDAY
6:00
7:00
8:00
9:00
10:00
11:00
12:00
1:00
2:00
3:00
4:00
5:00
6:00

SATURDAY
SUNDAY

To begin developing your calendar, place the weekly requirements from the time line in the Saturday spaces. For example, the requirements of the fifth week are placed on Saturday of the fifth week of the quarter, as shown in Figure 6-8. Leave the first line blank, and enter every activity — both academic and nonacademic — that is to be completed that week. In this example, the calendar shows the four history tasks to be completed during the fifth week, along with the fifth-week requirements from other courses (an English theme and a biology lab report). In addition, the calendar includes a reminder that your Aunt Jane's birthday is the following week, and you need to write her a letter.

FIGURE 6-8.
Use each Saturday page of your calendar to fill in the requirements for the upcoming week.

SATURDAY
1. Reading
2. Correct O.R.; final practice
3. Gather info for term paper
4. English theme; 5. Bio lab
6. Letter to Aunt Jane

Develop a calendar for each week as soon as you receive your assignments for the quarter or semester. Your weekly calendars should be completed by the end of the first week of the term.

THE DAILY CALENDAR

The successful student does some work in each course every day and still has time for other activities. The key to this success is keeping daily calendars that direct your efforts each day. Every Saturday, complete daily calendars for each day of the upcoming week.

The example in Figure 6-9 is for Tuesday of the fifth week of the quarter. First, place your class schedule for the day on the calendar. Second, record any other appointments or commitments you have that day — any time requirements that are not related to your classes. For instance, since you wish to write a birthday letter to Aunt Jane, you should buy the card early in the week; Tuesday would be an appropriate day to make the purchase. You should also note your plans to have lunch with your friend Fred and to attend a concert at 7:30 PM in the fine arts building.

The final step in completing your daily calendar is entering your study requirements for the day. Refer to the tasks on your weekly calendar, spreading them out over the week so that

FIGURE 6-9.
A sample daily calendar page. Fill in assignments first, then other commitments.

TUESDAY	
6:00	
7:00	
8:00	
9:00	English 101
10:00	
11:00	Biology 100
12:00	
1:00	
2:00	History 101
3:00	
4:00	Biology Lab
5:00	
6:00	

TUESDAY	
6:00	
7:00	
8:00	
9:00	English 101
10:00	
11:00	Biology 100
12:00	Lunch with Fred
1:00	
2:00	History 101
3:00	
4:00	Biology Lab
5:00	Buy birthday card
6:00	Dinner at snack bar
7:30	Concert, fine arts bldg

you accomplish some tasks each day (see Figure 6-10). Make sure you include prime study time. Each day, the top priority for your calendar should be to review all the notes you have taken that day and the day before. This review only requires a few minutes — about 5 minutes per class. Also leave time for the other elements of prime study time — preparing to listen in class the next day, making study cards, and reviewing your back notes.

FIGURE 6-10.
Sample calendar page with study time blocked in.

TUESDAY	
6:00	
7:00	
8:00	
9:00	English 101
10:00	Review notes, make study cards, prepare to listen
11:00	Biology 100
12:00	Lunch with Fred
1:00	Practice oral report
2:00	History 101
3:00	Gather T.P. info
4:00	Biology Lab
5:00	Buy birthday card
6:00	Dinner at snack bar
7:30	Concert, fine arts bldg

Recall that your weekly calendar for the fifth week includes the tasks shown in Figure 6-8. Suppose that on Monday of that week, you plan to accomplish the following tasks: (1) reading, (2) oral presentation corrections and practice, and (3) gather information for term paper. For Tuesday you should be able to (2) practice the oral report and (3) spend another hour gathering data for the term paper. Your Tuesday calendar will appear as shown in Figure 6-10.

As mentioned earlier, you should view your schoolwork as a career. By spreading out your work across the available time each day, you should be able to complete all tasks between 8:00 AM and 5:00 PM, the hours of a regular job.

CALENDARS AS CHECKLISTS

Daily calendars should serve both as schedules and as checklists. Follow them religiously, and at the end of each day, check to see if all tasks have been completed. If any have not, attempt to complete them the following day. Using the daily calendar in this way, you should never get behind on your academic tasks or on the daily study that is so crucial for academic success.

A further check of your progress is the weekly calendar. The weekly calendar is designed to guide you both in developing your daily calendars and in monitoring your completed tasks. Just as you check your daily calendar each day, review your weekly calendar each Saturday. At that time, determine whether you completed all tasks for the past week, and develop your daily calendars for the upcoming week. The calendars in our example might be checked as shown in Figure 6-11. In this example, you checked off all the tasks for Tuesday of the fifth week, but at the end of the week, you still need to gather more information for your term paper. This task should be placed as the top priority for week 6.

One of the main problems in completing your tasks each day is that others wish to see you, and they use up your time. If this becomes a problem for you, consider arranging to meet people for lunch or dinner. This act shows consideration for others, but still leaves you time to complete your assigned tasks each day.

No other academic asset is as important as a carefully managed day. Academic work is a daily task, not one of fits and starts. For more advice on managing your time and effort, we recommend *How to Get Control of Your Time and Your Life,* by Alan Lakein. This book is very straightforward and very useful.

FIGURE 6-11.
As you complete a task, check it off. Uncompleted tasks become a priority for next week.

TUESDAY	
6:00	
7:00	
8:00	
9:00	English 101
10:00	✓ Prime study time
11:00	Biology 100
12:00	Lunch with Fred
1:00	✓ Practice oral report
2:00	History 101
3:00	✓ Gather T.P. info
4:00	Biology Lab
5:00	✓ Buy birthday card
6:00	Dinner at snack bar
7:30	Concert, fine arts bldg

SATURDAY	
✓	1. Reading
✓	2. Correct O.R.; final practice
	3. Gather info for term paper
✓✓	4. English theme; 5. Bio lab
✓	6. Letter to Aunt Jane

TIME MANAGEMENT REVIEW QUESTIONS

1. Why do you think time management is the most important skill for college students? Why is it so much more important for college students than for high school students?

2. Why must you know what your assignments and deadlines are for you to manage your timed?

3. What is the purpose of the time line?

4. How many courses should your time line cover?

5. What are the steps of the academic process?

6. How do you apply these steps to the time line?

7. What is the purpose of the weekly checklist?

8. Should you plan to do most of your studying during the day or at night?

9. What is the purpose of the daily checklist?

10. Why do you plan your daily checklists on a weekly basis?

11. Explain the most important reason for planning a term's work.

12. What is the most important activity to be scheduled each day?

TIME MANAGEMENT EXERCISES

1. You are taking freshman English. Your assignments for the term include the following:

    a. Eight five-paragraph essays are required. The essays will count 40% of your grade.

    b. Every other week you are to submit a summary of essay readings. The readings will count 20% of your grade.

    c. A term paper is to be completed by the 15th week of the term. It will count 20% of your grade.

    d. The final exam will be the last week of the term. It will count 20% of your grade.

    Prepare a time line to accomplish all assignments.

2. Develop a daily checklist to be completed by 6:00 with the following schedule:

    8:00 AM – English

    9:00 AM – Physical Education

    10:00 AM –

    11:00 AM –

    12:00 PM – Lunch

    1:00 PM – Chemistry

    2:00 PM – History (1 hr.)

    3:00 PM –

    4:00 PM – Chemistry Lab

    5:00 PM – Dinner (1 hr.)

    The schedule should include reviewing notes, making study cards, writing an outline for an English essay, completing 25 pages of history reading, and working in the chemistry lab.

TIME MANAGEMENT SUMMARY

Managing your time is the single most effective way to control and manage your life. In managing your time, it is recommended that you use the following types of preparation:

1. Develop a time line.

   a. Obtain a schedule of when each class meets, and a list of assignments for each class.

   b. Place the due dates for your assignments on the time line.

   c. Divide long-term assignments into parts, according to the steps of the academic process: selecting a topic, gathering information, organizing the information, developing an outline, preparing the final draft or presentation, editing or correcting, and preparing the final report.

   d. Place the steps on the time line, beginning with the last step in the process and working toward the beginning.

2. Develop weekly and daily calendars.

   a. When you receive your assignments for the quarter or semester, develop weekly calendars by placing your weekly requirements in the Saturday spaces.

   b. Every Saturday, complete daily calendars for each day of the upcoming week.

   c. In addition to your classes and assignments, record any other appointments or commitments you have for each day — any time requirements that are not related to your classes. Refer to the tasks on your weekly calendar, and spread them out over the week so that you accomplish some tasks each day.

3. Use your calendars as checklists.

   a. At the end of each day, check to see if all the tasks on your daily calendar have been completed. If any have not, attempt to complete them the following day.

   b. Review your weekly calendar each Saturday. Determine whether you completed all tasks for the past week, and develop your daily calendars for the upcoming week.

CHAPTER 7

Concentration

Concentration is focal attention with awareness — the ability to focus on a single object, idea, concept, or problem, while remaining aware of what is going on around you. Concentration is needed to perform any conscious act. Even acts that appear to be entirely physical require considerable concentration. Have you ever noticed how announcers at sporting events often speak about an athlete's ability or lack of ability to concentrate? For example, if a wide receiver drops a pass thrown right into his hands, or if a pitcher begins to throw balls rather than strikes, the announcer may blame the mistakes on poor concentration. The mental components of these acts are at least as vital to success as their physical components. Concentrating is even more critical for mental acts such as listening, reading, note taking, test taking, and other forms of academic effort.

Most students are only able to concentrate for very short periods. It is not uncommon for students to be able to concentrate for just 90 to 120 seconds. Fortunately, you can learn to concentrate much longer, and possibly much more deeply. Next to improving your listening and your use of prime study time, improving your concentration is the best way to improve your time use. Improved concentration allows you to perform at a much higher level with considerably less effort. It's a little like improving the mileage that your car gets.

Most people assume that the ability to concentrate is innately determined, and that you can't do much to change it. In the minds of many, concentration is related to intelligence. Many great geniuses, such as Einstein and Newton, have been noted for their ability to concentrate for long periods of time, until a problem had been solved. (Einstein could concentrate for up to 2 hours at a time.)

Fortunately, it's not just the great geniuses who are able to operate with a high percentage of their ability for sustained amounts of time. While geniuses may have been born with an advantage, many people whose concentration is strikingly good have trained themselves to concentrate.

With practice, you can concentrate for up to 10 or 20 minutes, and perhaps longer. At that level, you will find that it takes much less "quality time" to do excellent work. It's as if you could, by practice, make yourself smarter. All of us have much greater mental ability than we use. Concentration allows us to focus more of our mental resources on whatever it is we're doing.

The steps toward improving your concentration are relatively simple and straightforward.

- Find an appropriate study place, as described earlier.

- Consider listening to quiet music on headphones. Tapes of "white noise" — ocean, sea, surf, or meadow sounds that block out external noise (TV, traffic, etc.) — can be very helpful. Alternatively, you could purchase a sound generator designed to block out distractions.

- Buy a clock with a second hand or a digital seconds display.

- Set definite times for how long you plan to work. Try to work in short stretches, 20 minutes or so at a time (30 minutes tops).

- Between 20-minute segments, be sure to take a real break. If you're making a concerted effort to concentrate, you'll be tired and ready for a break at the end of 20 minutes.

As you prepare to concentrate, try to empty your mental foreground, to clear your mind of everything but the material you're working on. Identify thoughts that are likely to distract you, and make a conscious note that for your 20 minutes of concentration, you will postpone these thoughts — you will focus solely on the material at hand.

If you feel yourself beginning to get distracted, resist by repeating the word "No!" and relentlessly pulling yourself back to the material. (This is an old trick from meditation.) As you finally get distracted, check the clock to see how much time has elapsed. At first, the process is likely to be quite discouraging. Ordinary students will find that they can concentrate for just a minute or two, and it will take some time for them to build up their concentration to 4 or 5 minutes. But after your concentration begins to improve, it builds rather quickly.

Keep a record of your times — particularly your best times, so that you're shooting for your personal best. Try to concentrate a little bit longer each time. It helps to keep a chart, either on a computer or with pencil and paper.

Watch your learning improve as your concentration times improve. You'll find that as you concentrate longer, you'll be concentrating better and getting more out of your reading. You'll also find that your memorization becomes smoother and more effective.

If you concentrate each day, recording and comparing your concentration times, you will find that your concentration span steadily increases. Gradually, as your concentration improves, you'll be able to go the full 20 minutes without becoming distracted. You will find that your time is working better than ever before.

DIFFICULTIES WITH CONCENTRATION

Concentration can be maximized with persistence and effort, but the attempt to get better at concentrating will occasionally bring you into direct conflict with some of your oldest and worst study habits. Although nearly all of us have the potential to concentrate better, we have had years of practice in how *not* to concentrate. Often when we try to concentrate, we get distracted, we daydream, we think of things that need to be done right away instead of the things we were supposed to be concentrating on.

Distractions to our concentration come in all shapes and sizes, but there are two basic kinds — the internal distraction and the external distraction. Both can be devastating to any attempt to focus attention on an academic task.

The external distraction is easily understood. Any noise, sight, or other stimulus outside a learner's immediate vicinity can qualify as an external distraction. Sirens and cars' squealing brakes are good examples of street sounds that can distract almost anyone. Fireworks or gunshots will distract as well. Some students cite a crying infant or a nearby television as a concentration killer. Visual distractions are also tough to ignore. Photographs of loved ones and pictures or souvenirs that remind you of good times gone by are almost certain to be distracting. As we have pointed out, the way to deal with external distractions is to modify your study environment so that very few stimuli are present. By sharply limiting your visual and auditory fields, you will minimize your susceptibility to these distractions.

The internal distraction can be even more powerful than the external one. A good example of an internal distraction is the sudden realization, as you are settling down to concentrate, that you may have left something cooking on the stove. Other internal distractions include remembering a telephone call you need to make, a bill that needs paying, a recent argument, or some other intense emotional experience.

The best way to deal with internal distractions is to use the technique from meditation that we discussed earlier: as you feel yourself becoming distracted, repeat aloud to yourself, "No, No, No." Visualize your concentration as a screen that you control, and move any would-be distraction off that screen. This method works pretty well most of the time, but occasionally you will be best served by just quitting whatever you are doing and tending to your distraction. Make the phone call, pay the bill, or take care of whatever else is bothering you. Some internal distractions are so powerful that no amount of effort at concentration can overcome them. In these cases, first deal with the distraction, and then get back to your concentration.

As you begin the long journey of improving your concentration, you will undoubtedly encounter both internal and external distractions. Keep a sense of humor, follow our instructions, and remember that if you persevere, your concentration *will* improve.

CONCENTRATION REVIEW QUESTIONS

1. What is "white noise"?

2. Give a short definition of concentration.

3. Why is it important to study in short (15- to 20-minute) stretches?

4. How does your intention to concentrate help you concentrate better?

5. How can you decrease distractions when you are trying to concentrate?

6. Why is it important to keep track of how long you can concentrate?

7. Why should you clear your mind when you are attempting to concentrate?

CONCENTRATION EXERCISES

1. Make a list of what distracts you when you are trying to concentrate. Areas you may consider include the following:

    a. Noise.

    b. Things you see.

    c. Thoughts that interfere with what you are trying to concentrate on.

    d. Temperature.

    e. Uncomfortable chair.

    f. Light or lack of it.

    After you have made the list, try to make a plan for overcoming those distractions. Decide what you should do about anything that interferes with your concentration. Be sure to keep a record of your concentration.

2. Practice the following procedure for improving your concentration.

    a. Begin by saying to yourself, "I will concentrate."

    b. Visualize your mental screen; you may think of it as resembling a television screen. This screen is the focus of your concentration. You have total control of what goes on the screen. Tell yourself that you have control of your concentration.

    c. Make the mental screen blank, and then put on the screen what you wish to concentrate on. (This may be something you are reading, studying, listening to, etc.)

    d. If your concentration wanes or you get distracted, try to decide what caused you to lose your concentration. Make a record of what distracted you and think about how to avoid letting it distract you again.

    e. Repeat steps a through d.

CONCENTRATION SUMMARY

Concentration is focal attention with awareness. It is needed to perform any conscious act, and particularly academic tasks. Most students are only able to concentrate for very short periods. Fortunately, almost anyone can improve his or her concentration, following several simple suggestions:

1. Find an appropriate study place, with a clock in view.

2. Listen to quiet music or white noise on headphones.

3. Set definite times for how long you plan to work (20 to 30 minutes at a time). Take breaks between the segments.

4. Clear your mind of everything but the material you're working on. Identify and postpone distracting thoughts.

5. If you begin to get distracted, repeat the word "No!" Visualize your field of concentration as a screen, and move potential distractions off that screen.

6. As you finally get distracted, check the clock to see how much time has elapsed.

7. Keep a chart of your times, and try to concentrate a little bit longer each time.

CHAPTER 8

Managing Your Learning

Managing your learning refers to the actions you can carry out that affect the way you process information. The primary methods we will explain in this chapter are the structuring of information and the daily review of material.

DEVELOPING STRUCTURES

Human beings learn and structure information better than any other creatures. We learn automatically, whether we want to or not. All day long, we categorize, classify, and file away information, from TV commercials and useless gossip to Shakespeare.

In school, you mostly learn through associations — associating new ideas, concepts, and definitions with those you already know. These associations are tied together into structures, bodies of ideas that fit together. The structures of information that most people are familiar with include history, math, science, language, and other fields. Within each of these large structures are many layers of smaller structures.

The brain is constantly developing structures for information to enable it to store the material encountered in daily activity. When you are preparing for a lesson, listening in class, or taking notes, try to organize the material into groupings — determine what kinds of information, feelings, concepts, and facts go together, and in what ways. Developing these conceptual structures in the classroom helps you to recall the material whenever the knowledge is needed. We remember stories that hang together, but we forget extraneous details. Once you assemble conceptual structures of information, you can integrate ideas (including the details you might otherwise forget) into a coherent, meaningful whole. These integrated ideas and details will be much easier to retrieve.

DAILY REVIEW

After you have created structures, the best way to commit facts, ideas, and concepts to memory is by constant review. A basic principle of remembering academic material is that *you recall what you see often over time.* Anything that you see, hear, smell, feel, or taste frequently over time, you tend to remember — without even trying. In school, or in any other structured setting, you can use automatic learning to your advantage. Daily review of notes and study cards capitalizes on this learning, the way the brain naturally functions. For this reason, it is one of the easiest methods of study.

Reviewing your notes involves carefully reading through them and concentrating on their content; do not try to memorize them. After you take a set of class or reading notes, *review them every day for at least 5 consecutive days.* After that point, continue to review the notes once a week until the recall of that content is no longer required.

As with notes, study cards are to be reviewed, not studied. Carry your cards with you all the time, and try to *look at each card 5 or 6 times a day,* with at least one hour between each viewing. Study 5 to 10 cards at a time. Try to review your study cards during down time — when you're waiting for a bus, waiting for a class to start, or in line for lunch — any time you have a few moments. This way, you make effective use of time that might otherwise be wasted.

At the end of the day, you should be able to look at either side of a card and recite the opposite side. Place the cards you know in a separate stack. If you cannot recall a card after one day of review, carry that card another day. *Once a week, review all your cards.* This type of review maintains optimum recall throughout the time memory of a detail is needed.

The purpose of study cards is to identify the detailed material that is likely to be questioned on a test and to give you a chance to remember the information precisely. Study cards isolate the information you need to know. If you try to memorize items from a page of notes, textbook page, or study sheet, you can't help seeing the rest of the information on the page. On a study card, these distractions are eliminated.

The cards keep you from kidding yourself. Most students who encounter trouble on tests have persuaded themselves that they knew the material when they really didn't; *they understood it, but they lacked the detailed knowledge that would have gotten them A's.*

Daily review may also be accomplished using what is known as an audio study card. To make an audio study card, first make a list of the details you wish to learn in this manner. Appropriate details include those used on regular study cards — a term with its definition, an event with its date, a formula with its use, a question with its answer, and so on. After you have collected the material, place a blank tape in the tape recorder. Push the Record button and state into the microphone the item to be learned (the event, formula, question, etc.). Let the recorder continue to record as you silently read the definition or identification (date, use, answer, etc.). This leaves a gap of silence on the tape. Then repeat the item and its identification or definition out loud.

To study from the tape, listen to each item, and during the pause that follows, recite the definition or identification. The tape will then repeat the item and provide the correct response. This technique allows you to learn material as you practice tennis, mow the lawn, or carry out any number of other activities that require little thinking.

The tape recorder can also be used to record more complicated concepts, main points, and other interrelated pieces of information. This technique is somewhat different from the use of audio study cards. It involves organizing the information and recording it so you can listen to it at times when the review of notes is not possible. Examples of topics that may be studied in this manner are law cases, pharmacology information on drugs, concepts and relationships in history, and any number of other areas involving a great deal of interrelated information.

Audio tapes are also useful for reviewing material in another setting, *relaxed review.* Organize the information, record it on a tape, and then listen to the tape while relaxed. Relax on a sofa or bed in a reclined position, thinking relaxing thoughts. Then begin to listen to the tape. It is not necessary to concentrate on the tape; you can even continue to think relaxing thoughts. Some students have found that playing relaxing music while listening to taped information is especially helpful.

Relaxation review involves three very useful learning modes: organizing, reciting, and reviewing information. Overall, relaxation review is both a pleasant and effective way to learn academic matter.

LEARNING MANAGEMENT REVIEW QUESTIONS

1. What is a learning association?

2. What is a learning structure?

3. How do structures and associations help you learn material?

4. What is the basic principle of remembering academic material?

5. How often should you review your study cards?

6. What is an audio study card?

7. What type of information is best learned by using a study card?

8. How many items of information should you try to put on each study card?

9. Explain what is entailed in relaxed review.

LEARNING MANAGEMENT EXERCISES

1. Make study cards from the following sentences.

    a. The formula for the area of a circle is 22/7 multiplied by the square of the radius of the circle.

    b. Columbus discovered America in 1492.

    c. A *calyx* is a ring of sepals at the base of a flower.

    d. If two negative integers are multiplied together, the product is positive.

    e. Newton's first law of motion states, "If there is no net force acting on a body, it will continue in its state of rest or will continue moving along a straight line with uniform speed."

2. Use the same sentences to make audio study cards.

3. **ADVANCED EXERCISE**

    Devise a strategy for creating structures of knowledge that you find to be useful to you as you study. Possible methods include outlines, graphs, charts, and pictures. Go through a chapter in one of your textbooks and use the method you have chosen to structure the information. You should expect to have five to nine categories, with at least five subsets in each category. After you have developed one method for structuring the information in the chapter, choose another method and compare the effectiveness of the two. In the future, consider many ways to structure what you are learning.

LEARNING MANAGEMENT SUMMARY

To improve the effectiveness of your learning and memory, you should develop structures for your knowledge and engage in daily review.

1. **Developing Structures.** You learn automatically, associating new ideas, concepts, and definitions with the ideas you already know. These associations are tied together into structures, bodies of information composed of ideas that fit together. You can support this function by prestructuring related information during class, in your mind and in your notes. Developing structures helps you to recall ideas, as well as the details associated with them, whenever the knowledge is needed.

2. **Daily Review.** Daily review of material is the best recall method for structured information. *You recall what you hear or see often over time.* Several types of daily review are described below.

    a. Notes

    -   Review your notes from lectures and reading every day for 5 days.

    -   Review all notes at least once a week.

    b. Study cards

    -   Review 5-10 at a time, 5 to 6 times per day.

    -   Leave an hour between each review.

    -   Place the cards you know in a separate stack.

    -   Once a week, review all your cards.

    c. Audio study cards

    -   Make a list of the details you wish to learn.

    -   Press Record and state the item to be learned, silently read the definition or identification, then repeat the item and its identification out loud.

    -   To study, listen to each item, and during the pause that follows, recite the definition or identification.

d. Recording of complicated ideas

- Organize the information you wish to learn and record it.

- Listen to the tape when you have no time to review your notes.

- Use this method for law cases, pharmacology information, concepts and relationships in history, etc.

e. Relaxed review

- Organize the information you wish to learn and record it.

- Listen to the tape while in a reclined position, thinking relaxing thoughts, and playing additional background music if you wish.

CHAPTER 9

Managing Your Memory

The main problem most students face with memory is one of *recall* — the ability to retrieve information from memory when you need it. Intention alone improves recall; simply intending to remember will improve your concentration, your mental processing, and therefore, your ability to recall the material. In addition, there are several specific techniques designed to enhance recall and improve your performance on academic work.

CATEGORY METHOD

Often it is necessary for you to recall a list of items. One useful approach for such tasks is categorizing the items, using the following steps:

1. Go through the list and determine how the various items are alike and different.

2. Organize like items into categories.

3. Number the categories.

4. Determine the number of items in each category.

5. Review the items by category several times, noting the number of items in each category.

Then, when you need to recall the list, use the following procedure:

1. Recall the number of categories and repeat the category names in your mind.

2. Recall the number of items in the first category, and then recall each item in

that category. Knowing how many items are in a category makes it much easier to recall the list. Your recall also improves because you are trying to recall a relatively small list.

3. Go through the other categories, recalling the items in each one. Your recall will improve greatly.

LOCI METHOD

Another technique to use for recalling long lists is called *loci.* The *loci* method was developed by the Greeks many centuries ago. In this procedure, you associate each item on a list with a particular place. This type of recall method is used by some instructors at the beginning of each term. If students sit in assigned seats, according to a seating chart, the instructor can identify each student by his or her location. By looking at the chart, the instructor can find the name of the student seated in the fourth seat of the second row, or anywhere else in the class. After only a short time, he or she will have learned all the students' names by associating each name with a seat location.

There are several ways you can employ the *loci* method. Suppose you are required to learn the names of the United States presidents, in order. Your first task is to pick a place you know exceptionally well. You may choose your home, since you are very knowledgeable about its layout. Imagine that your home has an entrance foyer leading to the living room, which leads to the dining room, then the den, and finally the kitchen. With this arrangement in mind, visualize placing the presidents in order in seating places throughout your house. You may place George Washington in the chair in the foyer and John Adams in the first seat on the living room sofa, next to Thomas Jefferson. Continue to visualize placing each president in order throughout your home. Go over this placement in your mind and review it several times.

When you are called upon to recall the presidents in order, visualize the arrangement of your home, and then visualize where you placed each president. Recall each one by associating the president's name with his location. Some students find it helpful to write each president's name on a 3 x 5" index card and place the card on a sofa or chair. This provides you with a more tangible act to recall. You may then go back and retrieve each card, reinforcing the association. When you are asked to name the presidents in order, visualize going back to your house and picking up the cards.

A combination of the *loci* and category methods can be particularly useful with long lists. In the above example, you can divide the presidents into three or four categories. For instance, you may have one category for all presidents prior to Andrew Jackson, another category for all presidents from Jackson through Grover Cleveland's second term, a third category from Cleveland through Harding, and a final category for the remainder of the presidents. After counting the number of presidents in each category, associate each of the four groups with a particular room. You could put the first group in the living room, the second group in the dining room, and so on. This technique helps you to recall the presidents in order, and gives you the added advantage of breaking the list into smaller, more manageable units.

MNEMONIC DEVICES

Mnemonic devices assist your memory by associating a word or sentence with another word, group of words, or sentence. They are particularly helpful in recalling short lists. Below we describe several examples of mnemonic devices. Each example is a type of *epynym,* a word or group of words designed to help you remember other words.

HOMES is a mnemonic device for the Great Lakes. Note that *HOMES* is comprised of the first letters of each lake (Huron, Ontario, Michigan, Erie, and Superior). *Every Good Boy Does Fine* is used in the study of music. The first letter of each word represents a note that falls on a line of the treble clef. Similarly, the letters in *FACE* represent the notes that fall between the lines on the treble clef.

Note that the last two mnemonic devices both help you to recall the names of notes, but do so in different ways. *FACE,* like *HOMES,* is an *acronym* — a single word that represents the first letters in other words in a series (counting the names of notes as separate words). *Every Good Boy Does Fine* is an *acrostic* — a sentence in which the first letter of every word represents the first letter in another word. Sentences can also be used to represent people, objects, and other items. For instance, the sentence *My Very Educated Mother Just made Sandwiches for Us of Nutritious Peanut butter* can be used to learn the planets of the solar system (Mercury, Venus, Earth, Mars, Jupiter, Saturn, Uranus, Neptune, and Pluto).

When creating an acrostic, it is helpful to use the names of people you know and to make the sentence funny. The more ridiculous you make the sentence, the easier it will be to recall. While mnemonics aid your recall and improve your performance on tests, they can also make your studying fun.

Mnemonics can be used in combination with the category and *loci* methods. For instance, a sentence could be constructed for each category of presidents; the first letter of each president's name would be the first letter in a word in one of the mnemonic sentences.

BOTTOM-UP LEARNING

One of the most difficult tasks for many students is learning a poem — especially if the poem is to be recited in front of the class or the instructor. Recall is almost always difficult, and it becomes even more difficult with the added stress of having an audience.

A very effective way to memorize a poem is to learn it from the bottom up. First, read all the way through the poem, and learn the last line. Next, read through the poem and learn the next to last line. Then, read it through and learn the third line from the bottom (still recalling the last and the next to last lines). Continue this procedure until you have learned the entire poem. This should happen around the point when you have intentionally learned the last half of the poem; since you go over the entire poem with each reading, you learn the first half automatically.

Bottom-up learning helps you to learn a poem in about half the time it would take to learn it from beginning to end. It has the added advantage that when you are asked to recite, your reading improves toward the end of the poem. Usually, students' performance declines as they go on.

The bottom-up method is equally effective in learning prose. Simply divide the material into line lengths comparable to those in a poem. It is best for each line to make sense, but all the lines need not be sentences. After you have converted the prose into a poem-like format, use the bottom-up technique to commit it to memory.

LEARNING PICTORIAL INFORMATION

Students are often asked to learn pictorial or illustrated information, such as charts, graphs, slides, and pictures. In art classes, you may have to learn the names and descriptions of various works of art. In history and geography, you may be asked to learn maps, charts, and other pictorial data. This type of information is extremely difficult to organize and learn.

One way to learn pictorial information is similar to the way you solve jigsaw puzzles. When you work on a jigsaw puzzle, you do not try to solve it all at once; you do a little bit at a time, beginning with the outer edges and other outstanding features. When attempting to learn a map, a slide, or a picture, divide the material into quadrants. Visualize the picture being split in half — first by a vertical line, and then by a horizontal line. Then, visualize both of these lines simultaneously, dividing the material into four equal parts. Number each quarter.

Notice that the middle of the material is cut by the visualized lines. This is important, since you should not try to learn the middle of the picture. Although our eyes are usually drawn to the middle of a picture, that is the most difficult part to learn. One reason for this is that pictorial material is typically very uniform near the center. It is much easier to learn pieces that are quite different from each other, and the major differences in slides, maps, charts, and pictures usually occur at the extremities.

Scan each quarter of the material, working your way from the edges toward the center, and look for a feature that grabs your attention. If something catches your eye in the first quarter of a picture, make a note of the name of the picture and the fact that its most distinctive feature is in the first quarter. Then review the picture several times, paying attention only to the first quarter. After learning only one fourth of a slide, picture, chart, or graph, you will be able to name it and distinguish it from all others.

STANDARD MEMORIZATION MATRIX

As emphasized in the previous chapter, you learn by associating new information with information you already know. The Standard Memorization Matrix capitalizes on this type of learning. The matrix includes 26 nouns in alphabetical order, with one noun for each letter of the alphabet (see Figure 9-1).

FIGURE 9-1.
Memorization Matrix

apple	box	cat	dragon	elephant
flag	golf	hand	Indian	jail
king	lasso	monkey	needle	onion
piano	quarter	ring	snake	tree
underwear	violin	wig	x-ray	yo-yo
		zebra		

Suppose you need to memorize a list of 10 items — *clown, hairpin, spaghetti, marsh-mallow, bathing suit, bird, gorilla, shoe, cigar,* and *tuxedo.* You can employ the Standard Memorization Matrix to accomplish the task with ease. Relate each item to one of the first 10 items in the matrix; if you can, form a mental image of the two items that includes some action. For instance, you would relate the first item in the list, *clown,* to the first item on the matrix, *apple.* Create a mental picture of the clown eating an apple, throwing an apple, or being hit by an apple. Make the image as vivid as possible. If you do this with each of the 10 items, you will find that you can recall the entire list, without even studying, just by looking at the matrix. Try finishing this example; you should find it both easy and fun.

MANAGING YOUR MEMORY REVIEW QUESTIONS

1. What are three methods for learning a list?

2. Explain how to use mnemonic devices.

3. What does the word *loci* mean?

4. When using the category method, should you number the categories as well as the items in each category?

5. Should you combine any of the methods when learning a list? If so, how?

6. What does HOMES stand for? Which memory technique does it employ?

7. Explain the best method for learning the content of a microscope slide.

8. Why do you learn pictorial information from the corners rather than from the middle of the illustration?

9. What does it mean to divide an illustration into quadrants?

10. Explain how to use bottom-up learning with a poem. Why do you think this method is so effective?

11. Explain how to use the Standard Memorization Matrix.

MANAGING YOUR MEMORY EXERCISES

1. Follow the procedure outlined in this chapter to develop recall categories for the following list:

   Loaf of whole-wheat bread
   Pound of coffee
   Two pounds of hamburger meat
   Half gallon of milk
   Five pounds of sugar
   Head of lettuce
   Pint of light cream
   Pound of tofu
   Pound of sharp cheddar cheese
   Two pounds of yellow squash
   Dozen donuts
   Small loaf of rye bread
   Two sirloin steaks
   Can of green beans
   Pound of bologna
   Can of beets
   Four center-cut pork chops
   Dozen dinner rolls
   Dozen apples
   Head of cabbage
   Carton of cottage cheese

2. Use one of the categories you developed and create a mnemonic device to help you recall the items in that category.

3. Use the *loci* method to help recall another category you developed.

4. Tell one of your friends how to use bottom-up learning to memorize a poem.

5. Learn the first 10 words of the memorization matrix in order (A – J). This will be useful to you when you need to recall any list of 10 or fewer items.

CHAPTER 10

Class Participation as Process

The primary processing operations exercised during class are summarizing, questioning, developing associations, and participating during class discussions or small group activities. Each of these offers you improved recall of information and increased learning during class time. These mental activities also help improve listening and note taking skills.

SUMMARIZING

Summarizing involves determining the value of information and restating ideas in your own words. Summary processing is a much higher order of mental functioning than direct recall of information. It is a very effective and efficient way to gain understanding and to improve your memory. It is also a great way to get involved in the lecture.

Throughout class activities, you should question what is being said and done — not by raising your hand to seek an answer, but by silently making judgments about the material. The 5 *w*'s and the *h* — *who, what, when, why, where,* and *how* — are effective questions to ask as the class proceeds. Other effective questions include *What do I think the material means?, What could be the next idea?, What is the instructor driving at?, Why does the instructor emphasize that?,* and many others. Posing questions about the content makes the material more interesting and improves memory and learning.

DEVELOPING ASSOCIATIONS

The classroom is a useful place to develop associations. As the instructor is talking, good students attempt to form associations with the ideas presented. Asking yourself, *What do I already know that is similar to this material?* can help you improve your memory. For instance, associating the date of a new event with an event whose date you already know can help you remember the new date. You can employ this type of recall trick during a test or at any other time the new information is needed.

CLASS DISCUSSION AND SMALL GROUPS

Class discussions and small group interactions offer excellent opportunities to learn by talking. Talking to someone is a very effective means for improving recall. It requires high-order thinking, as you sort material into meaningful chunks of knowledge. As mentioned earlier, we recall about 22% of what we hear and 24% of what we see, but 76% of what we say and 94% of what we do. Talking is the best way to recall abstractions that cannot be performed. If class time does not provide an opportunity to talk about the material, schedule time to discuss it with someone.

CHAPTER 11

Test Preparation

The central problem you face in school is committing facts and ideas to memory so that you can reproduce them on tests. It is not enough simply to understand the material; it must be filed in your memory in such a way that you can retrieve it when you need it.

CRAMMING VS. DAILY REVIEW

To a large extent, test scores reflect the quality of your preparation. Test preparation should begin as early as possible; you should start studying for the final exam on the first day of class. Actually, you can start even earlier if you get the textbook(s) early. Listening in school and reviewing at home, develop your knowledge and understanding on a daily basis — day after day, one day at a time.

Follow the Golden 24-Hour Rule: *Do not attempt to learn any new material about the subject on which you will be tested during the 24 hours prior to the test.* Cramming on the night before a test is never truly effective. It often appears to work, and it may get you out of trouble, but material learned by cramming will rarely stay with you. Crammed material lacks the background and depth of understanding that characterize solid learning, so what is learned quickly is quickly lost; you may not remember what you crammed when you take the next test or discuss the material.

It takes time for your brain to structure information into categories. When you attempt to learn new material just prior to a test, you disrupt and disorganize the structures your brain has been creating over time. In contrast, when you allow your brain enough time to review, synthesize, and organize the material, learning becomes easy. Constant daily review of material delivers lasting results, and is consistently effective.

In the 24 hours prior to a test, instead of cramming, you should review all the material that the test will cover — including all your class notes, reading notes, study cards, graphic material, text, and any other material that could be on the test. If possible, review all of these materials in one sitting.

As you review, try to structure the information by considering questions such as the following:

- How is this material similar to other information I have learned?

- What are appropriate categories for this information?

- Does this information fit into any of my existing categories of knowledge?

- Is this detail information or abstract ideas?

- What is the best way to learn this information?

- How long will it take me to learn the information?

- What type of schedule should I develop?

These questions help you determine what kind of material you are trying to learn and what learning approach will support that type of content. This makes learning the information much easier, more efficient, and more effective. Two main types of information — details and general ideas — are discussed below.

DETAILS VS. THE BIG PICTURE

To perform well on tests, you need to know two types of information — the specific details of the course, and the "big picture" (the organization of the material, the way the material is structured, the overall meaning of the content, etc.).

To learn specific details, use your study cards; memorize all the cards for the segment of the course you're going to be tested on. (Review your study cards as often as you need to, so you remember all the details. Concentrate on the material to be covered on the test.) If you have taken good notes, know your cards cold, and really understand the general ideas in the material, you're unlikely to have trouble on the test. Test-taking troubles and anxiety typically follow people who don't memorize well and who don't know the relevant details. They may understand the big picture, but they lack detailed knowledge, and therefore can't answer tricky questions. Ambiguity gives them much trouble, because they lack the specific knowledge to resolve it.

In trying to understand the big picture, it helps to read all your notes at once. Other methods of gaining this broader understanding are described below.

1. Tell someone about the material. Trying to understand ideas well enough to tell someone about them, you get to know them quite well. For many students, this is the best method for gaining the big picture.

2. Organize the information into a structure that you can see, such as a picture or a diagram. One method is a *Venn diagram,* which consists of two or three overlapping circles (see Figure 11-1). Use each circle to represent a place, person, thing, or idea. If a feature or idea is associated with two or three circles, place it in the space where those circles overlap. A feature or idea related to only one circle should be placed in the part of that circle that does not overlap with any other circles. Other pictorial diagrams include the *tree diagram* — with the trunk as the main idea and the limbs as the supporting ideas (Figure 11-2) — and the *hierarchical diagram* (Figure 11-3).

3. Develop a brief outline of the material. This forces you to think through the ideas of the material, helping you understand the overall organization and structure of the content.

PRACTICE TESTS

Another extremely effective way to prepare for a test is to develop a practice test. Try to use the same general format as that of the actual exam. Whether or not you create a practice test, make it your business to know several facts about the exam — how many questions will be included, what kinds of questions they will be (essay, true/false, etc.), what general topics will be covered, whether you will be penalized for guessing, and how much time you will be given; if you do write up a practice test, use these facts as guidelines. If the instructor seems reluctant to provide these details, get the help of other students in requesting them. Frequently, an instructor does not want to give this type of information to just one student, but is willing to provide it to the entire class.

Determining the content of the questions is extremely important. Good sources of content for your practice test include class notes, notes from outside reading, textbooks, and any other information provided by the instructor. If you have been constructing questions during your daily review, these can form a nucleus for the practice test. Most instructor-made tests cover about one third of the content covered in class. Therefore, if you prepare three times the

FIGURE 11-1.
Venn Diagram

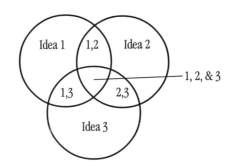

FIGURE 11-2.
Tree Diagram

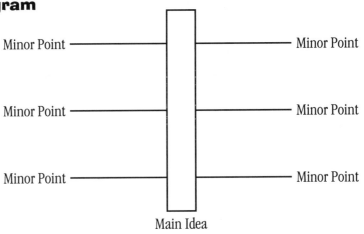

FIGURE 11-3.
Hierarchical Diagram

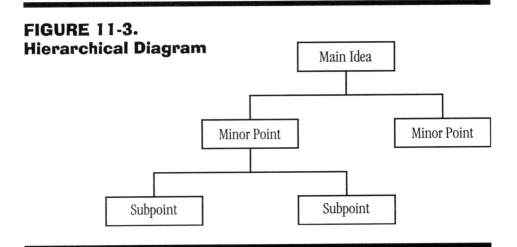

number of questions that will be on the test, you will come close to exhausting the content. Since that is a great deal of work, you may enlist two or more other students to help make up practice tests.

Students who try to predict test questions can be dazzlingly successful. You and a partner (or partners) can play games, trying to predict what the instructor will ask about. It can be helpful to look at old tests and ask people who have taken the course before what the tests were like; instructors tend to give the same kinds of tests over and over again. As you look over an old test, pay attention to how the questions are worded and what points the instructor emphasizes.

Once you are prepared for the format and general content of the test, you should be able to come up with a pretty good practice test. Try to figure out from the practice test what you *don't* know. If you and your friends make up tests for each other, try to stump each other. You will all learn a great deal about your weaknesses. And when you find weak spots, there will still be time to fix them.

Constructing and taking practice tests is one of the most effective methods of test preparation. It can often be overkill, however. If you know you are thoroughly prepared for a certain test, there is no need for you to prepare or take a practice test, though it will always be useful to try to predict the questions.

TEST PREPARATION REVIEW QUESTIONS

1. What is the Golden 24-hour Rule? Explain why it is important.

2. What are the two major types of information you must know if you are to perform well on a test?

3. Name at least three ways to learn the "big picture."

4. Why do you need to know several details about the test prior to taking it?

5. What is one of the best ways to learn the details of the course?

6. Are tests generally about details or the big picture?

7. What should you do the night before a test?

8. Why is preparing a practice test so effective?

9. Is it necessary to prepare a practice test for all tests? Why or why not?

10. What percent of the material covered is usually asked about on an instructor-made test?

11. Does cramming for a test usually work? Why or why not?

12. Should you talk to someone about a test while you are studying to take it?

13. Are students often able to predict what questions will be on a test? If so, how? If not, why not?

TEST PREPARATION EXERCISES

1. Prepare a Venn diagram showing the interactions among the processes in the following passage:

   "All forms of life grow and change, use energy, and reproduce. Growth and change require energy. The use and production of energy, in turn, requires change within life cells. Reproduction of cells requires both the use of energy and changes within cellular structure."

2. Could another method be used to organize the major points of the above information? If so, explain.

3. Develop a plan that provides step-by-step actions you would take to prepare for a test.

4. Develop a practice test for a chapter in one of your textbooks. If possible, use it to prepare for a real test.

5. Develop questions that will help you structure the information in a chapter in one of your textbooks.

6. Make at least 25 study cards for a chapter on which you will have a test. Learn these cards by carrying 5 to 10 around with you per day and reviewing each one at least five times, with a minimum of one hour between each review. If you learn 8 a day, you will be ready for the test in a week.

7. Teach a friend how to prepare for a test using what you have learned from this section and from your own experience.

TEST PREPARATION SUMMARY

1. Start studying on the first day of class — or earlier, if you can get the texts.

2. Find out as much as you can about the test (e.g., when it will be given, how much time you will have, what material will be covered, whether there are penalties for guessing, how many questions there will be, and what sort of questions they are).

3. Examine or ask about tests from previous years.

4. Review all the material that the test will cover — including your class notes, reading notes, study cards, graphic material, text, and any other material that could be on the test.

5. Try to structure the information by asking questions about it.

6. Determine what kind of information you are trying to learn and what learning approach will support that type of content.

   - To learn specific details, memorize your study cards.

   - To understand the big picture, read all your notes at once, tell someone about the material, organize the information in a picture or a diagram format, and develop a brief outline.

7. Create a practice test. Try to use the same general format and content as that of the actual exam, and try to prepare three times the number of questions that will be on the test.

CARDINAL RULES FOR PROCESS

1. You recall what you see often over time.

2. Spend some time every day on every subject.

3. It is always later than you think.

4. Everything takes time. Nothing is time-free.

5. Everything takes twice as long as you think it will.

6. Keep a weekly schedule and a daily calendar.

7. Review your notes every day for 5 days.

8. Learn the details. Overlearn the details.

9. Work in short stretches.

10. If you are concerned about a test, make up a practice test.

11. Think like the instructor.

12. Constant review of every course improves recall.

13. Set high goals, but set achievable short-range objectives that will help you meet your goals.

Output Skills

Output skills are often considered the most important study skills because they are typically observed, critiqued, graded, and reported. Your instructor sees your papers and tests, but does not see the hours of study and preparation that went into them. Often, output skills can be improved, with a consequent improvement in grades. Many a student studies hard but takes tests poorly, or makes careless errors on papers. These problems can be fixed fairly easily. We have found that most students can improve their test taking, writing, and oral reports, and that this improvement is quickly reflected in their grades. The output skills we will consider here include:

- **test taking,**
- **dealing with test anxiety,**
- **learning from tests,**
- **preparing written and oral reports,** and
- **participating in class.**

CHAPTER 12

Test Taking

The major output measure in school is usually the test or examination. Most of the time, you are graded primarily on the percentage of test questions you can answer correctly. As you progress in school, themes, essays, and papers become more and more important to your grades, but tests never disappear.

Follow the guidelines described in Chapter 11 to prepare for any test. Once the test time arrives, find a place to sit where you can't see anybody else well (a front corner of the room, for example). Begin to look over the test as soon as it comes to your desk. If it comes face down and you can't begin until all students have received a copy, count the number of pages.

When you can begin, preview the test. What types of questions are there? How many of each type are included? Get a feel for the test as a whole. Then read the instructions carefully. Decide how to respond on each section. Figure out how much each question is worth and make a schedule for yourself, leaving time to recheck your answers. For example, in a one-hour test you may spend 10 minutes on multiple-choice questions, 10 minutes on fill-in-the-blanks, 10 minutes on true/false questions, 20 minutes on essays, and 10 minutes checking over your answers.

THE TRIAGE METHOD

The term *triage* refers to a division into three parts or categories. In the case of test-taking, it means that you should go through the test and divide the questions into three groups: *probables,* the questions you can answer easily; *possibles,* the questions you think you can work out the answers to; and *long shots,* the questions you have no idea how to answer. Put a check by the possibles and an X by the long shots. As you go through the test, answer the probables first, and then come back to the checks and then the X's. Be sure to find out whether there's a penalty for guessing. If there is, you may not want to answer the long shots unless you can narrow the answer down to two possibilities.

Throughout the test, try to stay relaxed. To make use of your ingenuity — your ability to use creative thinking to figure out an answer you don't know — you have to keep your head. Never change your first guess unless you are certain you know the right answer. When you finish the test, review it for careless errors.

TRUE/FALSE QUESTIONS

True/false tests are easy to make and easy to grade. They are the favorite test type for many instructors. Strategies for answering true/false questions are listed below.

1. Beware of superlatives, such as *best, worst, largest, smallest, most, least,* etc. Few circumstances are *always* present. Equally few are *never* present. Remember that some actually are *always* or *never,* but be careful!

2. Check the statement for *qualifying words.* A qualifying word is any single word that changes the overall meaning of the statement. For instance, does the meaning of the statement change if the adjectives and adverbs are eliminated? Qualifying words are often keys to choosing the correct answer.

3. Look carefully at the subject and the verb in the statement. Do they belong together?

4. Be careful of reading too much into a statement. The more you know about a subject, the less you will see statements about the subject as true or false. Most statements are neither completely true nor completely false. Ironically, choosing between true and false becomes more difficult with broader knowledge. In one sense, the true/false test penalizes you for knowing more.

5. Try to prove each statement false. It is easier to prove a statement false than to prove it true. Every element in a statement must be true for the statement to be true. If just one element in a statement is incorrect, the statement is false. If you can find no error in a statement, accept it as true; don't try to prove it. This will keep you from reading too much into the statement.

MULTIPLE-CHOICE QUESTIONS

Multiple-choice questions are favored by more students than any other type. These questions do not tax your recall nearly as much as short-answer questions; they merely require you to select the answer from the choices provided. Well-designed multiple-choice questions can be difficult, however. In their ability to address very specific details — dealing with shades of meaning, conflicting information, appropriate conclusions, and other factors — multiple-choice questions are often challenging, even for very good students. To perform well on a multiple-choice test, you must know the relevant details and understand the meaning and context of that information. For this reason, and because multiple-choice tests are easy to grade, they are among the favorites of many instructors, as well as students. Every student should become a master of this type of question, especially since most standardized, nationally administered tests (such as the SAT, ACT, GRE, CSAT, MCAT, etc.) have a multiple-choice format.

Misconceptions about Multiple-Choice Questions

Many students think that the goal in answering a multiple-choice question is to get the right answer. This is untrue — multiple-choice questions require you to choose the *best* answer, not the correct one. All answers may be correct, or all may be incorrect; you are required to choose the best of these options. Therefore, you should always read every answer before giving a response. Don't automatically select the first correct answer you read, since another response may be better.

Many students also believe that you should choose a constant response when guessing on multiple-choice questions. Some suggest always guessing C, since more correct answers seem to be C than any other choice. This advice is misleading. When you're forced to guess, always try to make a knowledge-based guess. If you know *anything at all* about the subject, use that knowledge to narrow down the possibilities or to direct a hunch. Hunches are usually somewhat knowledge-based, and they will beat the odds of giving a constant response. However, if you have used all you know to narrow down the possibilities, and you still can't decide between two or more choices, you should use your knowledge of probability. On instructor-made tests, choices toward the end of the list are generally more likely to be correct than the ones toward the beginning (nationally standardized tests usually control for this factor). Therefore, if you absolutely can't decide between A and C on your instructor's test, it's better to go with C.

Another common misconception is that multiple/multiple-or-K questions work the same way as multiple-choice questions. A multiple/multiple-or-K question is one in which you are asked to select between possible combinations of responses — e.g., between (A), (A&B), (B), (B&C), (C), (A&C), (none of these), and (all of these). In this type of question, you are not being asked to select the best answer; you must select *all* of the correct answers. The appropriate strategy to use with these questions is to treat each statement as a true/false question. First try to prove that (A) is false. If you cannot prove it false, accept it as true and place a check by the (A) statement. Follow this pattern with the (B) and (C) statements, and then mark off the appropriate choice.

ESSAY QUESTIONS

Many students find essay questions difficult. Yet if you view the essay question as your opportunity to show off and prove what you know, with few constraints on what you say, these questions become much easier; the essay may even become your favorite type of question.

Essay questions become much easier and more enjoyable once you realize how they are graded. Many students dislike essay questions because they believe that the more they write, the better their grade will be. This is far from the truth. Typically, instructors predetermine the answers to each essay question. If the question asks you to explain three major causes of World War II and give illustrations of each, the instructor may decide that each cause is worth 25 points. Additional points would be given for examples and illustrations, and extra points could be awarded for exceptional answers.

The major point to understand is that the instructor is looking for very specific information from an essay. Your grade is determined by the amount of that information your essay provides. Grades on essay questions are no more arbitrary than grades on any other type of question.

Essay questions should be answered by following the Preacher's Method. The first paragraph of the essay should answer the question directly, telling the instructor what the essay will contain. If the question asks you to explain three major causes of World War II, the first paragraph should enumerate these causes in summary fashion. You should then devote at least one paragraph to each cause, giving a full explanation and several illustrations for each one. Finally, a paragraph that summarizes the essay should conclude your answer. Do not include other information about the war, or any other extraneous information.

SHORT-ANSWER QUESTIONS

Short-answer questions ask you to define a term, fill in the blank, complete a statement, or list specific items. These questions require you to recall the answer and provide no information other than the question. You are not choosing between responses, and the chance of guessing the correct answer is remote.

The best preparation for short-answer questions is to overlearn the details of the course. Extensive use of study cards is essential. If lists are covered by the short-answer questions, use *epynyms* (a word or group of words designed to help you remember other words) and other recall tricks, as described in Chapter 9. The best strategy for answering these questions is to first answer the *probables* (the answers you know cold) as quickly as you can. *Possibles* (the ones you might be able to get) should be answered next. *Long shots* (ones you have *no* idea about) may as well be left alone.

TEST TAKING REVIEW QUESTIONS

1. What does *triage* mean? What three types of test questions are identified in this process?

2. What steps should you follow when you take a test?

3. What strategies should you use when answering a true/false question?

4. Why do you need to read all the answers on a multiple-choice test?

5. Do you need to know the big picture to perform well on a multiple-choice test? Why or why not?

6. Explain what you should include in the first paragraph of an essay test.

7. Should an essay answer contain detailed information?

8. Why are true/false tests often unfair to students with the greatest amount of relevant knowledge?

9. Which type of short-answer test question usually takes the most time to answer?

TEST TAKING SUMMARY

The purpose of taking a test is to prove what you know. Principles of test taking are outlined below.

1. Be prepared. Follow the guidelines outlined in Chapter 11:

   a. Start studying on the first day of class.

   b. Find out as much as you can about the test.

   c. Examine or ask about tests from previous years.

   d. Review all the material that the test will cover.

   e. Try to structure information by asking questions about it.

   f. Determine what kind of information you are trying to learn and what learning approach will support that content type.

   g. If you are concerned about a test, create a practice test.

2. Follow a systematic procedure.

   a. If you must leave the test face down, count the pages.

   b. Once you can begin, preview the test. Get a feel for the test as a whole.

   c. Start the test. Read the instructions carefully, and decide how to respond.

   d. Make a schedule for yourself. Leave yourself time to check your answers.

   e. Use *triage*. Answer questions in the following order:

      * *probables* – questions you can answer easily;

      * *possibles* – questions you may be able to answer; and

      * *long shots* – questions about which you have no idea.

   f. Review the test for careless errors.

3. Learn strategies for specific question types: true/false; multiple choice; essay; and short answer.

CHAPTER 13

Avoiding Test Anxiety

Many students suffer from *test anxiety.* The degree of anxiety you suffer at test time can enhance or decrease your performance on the test. A little anxiety is useful in psyching you up. Too much anxiety psyches you out and greatly diminishes your performance.

Test phobia is quite different from test anxiety, and is not covered in this discussion. Test phobia is a deep-seated emotional problem that usually causes a student to avoid testing situations at all costs, and that requires long-term psychiatric care. Test anxiety is much less severe, and most students encounter it at one time or another. Some students seem to be anxious in nearly all testing situations, while others rarely experience the syndrome.

Anxiety is the body's method of dealing with situations that may cause personal harm. It is a defense mechanism that elicits both a physical response and a mental or emotional change. When people become anxious, their adrenaline flows, a large supply of oxygen travels to their arms and legs, and they experience what is known as a *fight or flight* response: they are physically and emotionally prepared to either fight or run from danger. A high level of anxiety allows us to perform unbelievable physical feats, but decreases our mental functioning considerably. During an attack of anxiety, oxygen that normally travels to the brain is transmitted to the limbs. Without its usual supply of oxygen, the brain loses a degree of its functioning capability.

To avoid anxiety, you should understand what causes anxiety to occur, how to control the situations that foster the response, and what to do if anxiety strikes.

CAUSES OF ANXIETY

To some extent, test anxiety is always caused by the individual. Tests may trigger anxiety, but they do not really *cause* it; different people react to tests in different ways. The following questionnaire can help you determine the extent to which you are susceptible to test anxiety. Answer *true* or *false* to each question:

1. The palms of my hands often become sweaty prior to or during a test.

2. My vision is sometimes blurred during a test.

3 Tests frequently have trick questions designed to make me do poorly.

4. I often know more about a subject than I am able to show on a test.

5. Tests are unfair because they require you to perform for just one hour when many hours of learning were necessary. Most tests are unfair.

6. During tests I often think about what will happen to me if I do poorly.

7. I really study but somehow I just don't do well.

If you answered *true* to four or more of these questions, test anxiety may be a problem for you. You need to understand what triggers your anxiety and how your actions influence the anxiety response. The *ABC*s of anxiety help to explain this process.

A is an *Activating situation.* For anxiety to occur, you must encounter a situation in which you or something you hold dear may be harmed. A test is certainly an activating situation. You could lose a chance to attend the college of your choice, or fail to qualify for some program or profession. An even greater harm is possible because a test may cause you to feel stupid. Few feelings are more damaging.

C is a *Condition of anxiety.* When you're anxious, your thought processes are diminished. On a test, you may not be able to recall facts, organize thoughts, analyze and summarize information, or develop conclusions. You need all these functions to perform well on tests.

You do not advance directly from *A* to *C.* The situation itself does not create anxiety. The mediating factor is *B* — what you *Believe* about the consequences of the situation. To avoid test anxiety, you must be in control of what you think. If you think of a test as an opportunity to show off and prove how much you know, anxiety is unlikely to strike. If you think of a test as possibly causing you to fail, as having a major negative impact on your future, anxiety will probably occur.

PREVENTING ANXIETY

To avoid anxiety, you must be in control of what you think. Several processes can help you to gain this control.

First, you should be prepared. Nothing creates confidence like knowing the material. Remember that knowing is not the same as understanding; while understanding is important, the test is on *details*. Anxiety often occurs when a student understands the material, but finds that the test asks about small details. Prevent anxiety by overlearning the details of the course. You can generally master details by using study cards extensively.

You should also develop a strategy for taking the test. The strategies described in Chapter 12 put you in control of the test situation. For instance, labeling the test questions as *probables, possibles,* and *long shots* allows you greater control over each question. Use ruthless time control and make your own schedule. When you develop a schedule beyond the one provided for the test — determining how much time to spend on each section or question — the control of time is shifted from the instructor to you. Taking control of all elements of the test decreases the possibility of an anxiety attack.

In addition to taking control over the test, you should take control over your own fears and expectations. Success comes to those who seek it, expect it, and visualize it before the event. Sit down and think about how the test will occur. Visualize yourself using strategies and doing well on the test. See yourself doing the best in the class. At test time, carry out the success you visualized. Taking practice tests is another way to build expectations of success. When you perform well in practice, you generally expect to perform well during the actual event. Practice is an effective way to overcome anxiety in almost any situation.

Often, good-luck charms are also effective. If you have a coin minted in the 1800s and everything seems to go well when you have it with you, take it to the test. Good luck comes to those who work hard, but also to those who expect to have good luck. Bring with you anything — a process, piece of clothing, gadget, etc. — that you feel encourages good luck. Praying, meditating, or repeating mantras may also help. Silently saying short familiar prayers or closing your eyes for a few seconds of private meditation can help you focus and relax.

ALLEVIATING ANXIETY

What should you do if you realize you are anxious while taking a test? Your palms are sweaty. Your vision is blurred. You begin to think there is no way to pass.

You have to stop, step back, and try to relax. Think about the test questions, not the consequences of the test. Breathe deeply to improve the flow of oxygen to your brain. Recall your visions of success. If possible, leave the room and get fresh air. Then return and continue with the test. Check your time schedule and focus on your test strategy. Ask yourself if you are following the *triage* method. Assure yourself that you have time to complete the parts of the test that you are most sure of passing (the first two levels of *triage*). Answer the first question you know for sure, skipping all those you went over but didn't know. Complete all the questions you feel fairly confident about answering, and then go back to those you skipped. Do not second-guess your answers.

It is important to recognize that occasionally, anxiety may strike. If this happens, focus on your test strategy and on succeeding. Think of yourself as a winner, and you'll be one!

TEST ANXIETY REVIEW QUESTIONS

1. Does the testing situation cause test anxiety? Why or why not?

2. What are the *ABC*'s of anxiety?

3. What is the primary cause of anxiety?

4. What are the symptoms of test anxiety?

5. What is the most important action to take to avoid test anxiety?

6. Name three ways to control what you think about a testing situation.

7. Why is it important to have a good time schedule?

8. What types of physical changes occur when you become anxious?

9. Why are good-luck charms effective in anxiety-arousing situations?

10. What actions can you take to help alleviate test anxiety?

TEST ANXIETY EXERCISES

1. Develop a written plan for what you expect to do before and during your next test to avoid test anxiety.

2. Develop a written procedure of actions you will take if you ever become test anxious.

3. Explain to someone whom you know is test anxious how anxiety can be avoided or overcome if it occurs.

TEST ANXIETY SUMMARY

Test anxiety is very common, but it can be prevented and controlled. To avoid anxiety, you should understand what causes anxiety, how to control situations that foster anxiety, and what to do if anxiety strikes.

1. **Causes of anxiety: A + B = C**
   Activating situation + *Beliefs* = *Condition* of anxiety

2. **Preventing anxiety.** Several processes help you control thoughts that cause anxiety.

   a. Overlearn the details of the course.

   b. Develop a strategy for taking the test.

   c. Use ruthless time control and make your own schedule.

   d. Visualize success.

   e. Take practice tests.

   f. Use good-luck charms, prayer, or meditation.

3. **Alleviating anxiety.**

   a. If possible, leave the room and get fresh air. Then return and continue with the test.

   b. Breathe deeply to improve the flow of oxygen to your brain.

   c. Recall your visions of success.

   d. Focus on the test questions and your test strategy, not on consequences of the test.

   e. Check your time schedule.

   f. Ask yourself if you are following the *triage* method.

   g. Assure yourself that you have time to complete the parts you are most sure of passing.

   h. Answer the first question you know for sure, skipping all those you went over but didn't know (the long shots).

   i. Complete the questions you feel fairly confident about.

   j. Go back only to the ones you skipped. Do not second-guess your answers.

CHAPTER 14

Learning from Tests

A major purpose of taking a test is to learn from it. You want to do well, but you also want a test to teach you more about test taking so that you can ace the next test. Students usually want to forget about a test as soon as it's over, as though they believe that the material will never be needed again. Good students know that tests can be very useful learning experiences. Understanding the mistakes you've made gives you valuable insights for future tests, and helps give you a feeling of control; this control will help significantly in managing anxiety.

The moment you leave the classroom after taking a test, make some notes for yourself on what questions gave you trouble. When you get the test back, correct all errors and learn the corrected answers. Attempt to find out why you missed each question, and what sort of questions gave you trouble. You and your study partner will be able to determine what you studied correctly and where you went wrong. Keep each test and use it to help prepare for the next test, midterm, or final examination. Remember that instructors often repeat the same questions, or variations of the same. Try not to make the same mistake twice.

On multiple-choice questions, there are three ways of making a mistake. The Type 1 error is a careless mistake. When you see this kind of error on your paper, you groan and think, "How could I possibly have done this foolish thing?" There are many ways this can happen — if you accidentally add instead of subtract, misunderstand the problem, mark (b) when you meant to mark (c), and so on.

The classic example is writing the answer for #6 in the place for #7, the answer for #7 in the place for #8, and so on, until you miss many answers in a row. Fortunately, this mostly happens in bad dreams, but it does occasionally happen in the real world.

Since we're all human, we all make Type 1 errors from time to time. These mistakes are almost impossible to eliminate entirely. Fortunately, though, you can cut down on them. The first step is to find out that you're making them. When you analyze your test paper, count how many Type 1 errors you make and how you make them. If you're making more than one or two per test, you're making too many, and you should take special care to avoid them in the future.

A Type 2 error occurs when some skill or piece of knowledge is lacking — for instance, if you're asked to define the *calyx* and you really don't know what a calyx is. Finding this type of mistake is an indication that you didn't study the right information, or you didn't learn the definition well enough to answer that question. If *calyx* was not on one of your study cards, you need to expand your cards. If it was, and you still missed it, you need to spend more time learning the study cards. If you find you are making many Type 2 errors, you probably need to make many more study cards and/or expand the information on the ones you have. You may also need to take better notes and listen more effectively.

If you didn't have a study card for a question you missed, try to figure out why. Where was the information mentioned? Why didn't you or your partner pick up on it? That kind of analysis can help you significantly improve your performance on future tests.

Type 3 errors occur when you choose incorrectly. Many of us have missed questions on which we were debating between two answers and we picked the wrong one. Often, the main problem is a failure to track the thought processes of the person who devised the test. Some tests are designed with distracting answers, tricks to encourage students to get off track. What you have to do on a multiple-choice question is find the *best* answer. This can be very difficult, because the best answer for one instructor is not necessarily the best answer for another. Analyze *why* an instructor counted one answer right and a similar one wrong. Analyzing Type 3 errors can help you figure out how an instructor thinks. It may also tell you about the specificity of your knowledge; sometimes, a Type 3 error is really a Type 2 error in disguise — if you'd known the material somewhat more thoroughly, you would not have missed the question.

TEST-TAKING RECORD

The Test-Taking Record (Figure 14-1 on the next page) is a very effective device for learning from each test. The information from every test, whether you received an *A* or an *F*, should be recorded on this chart.

FIGURE 14-1.
Test-Taking Record.

Subject of Test	Kind of Question	Type of Error	Solution	Grade	
				Test	Skill (1-10)

Directions

1. Copy Figure 14-1 (either with a photocopier, by hand, or on your computer), and record the name of the tested subject.

2. In the second column, determine the kind of question you missed (e.g., true/false, multiple-choice, essay).

3. In the third column, record the type of error you made. Types of error include careless mistakes, misunderstanding the question, not knowing the answer, overlooking the question, and any other type of error that caused the response to receive no credit.

4. In the fourth column, record the solution for correcting the error. This is a crucial step in learning from the test — if you do nothing about your errors, you will continue to make the same mistakes. Record what you plan to do to keep from making the same type of error on future tests. Possible solutions include making more study cards, reviewing notes more often, taking better notes, attending all classes, completing reading assignments, being more attentive in class, allowing more time for review, practicing a certain type of question, and many others.

5. There are two separate columns under *grade*. In the first of these columns, record the grade you received on the test. In the second column, give yourself a grade from 1 to 10 on how well you followed the test-taking strategy. You may arrive at this score by dividing your test strategy into five steps and giving yourself a score of 0–2 for each one. For instance, if you previewed the test, determining the number of each type of question, you earn 2 points for that part of the strategy. If you read the instructions and followed them carefully, you earn 2 more points. If you developed and followed a schedule, you again earn 2 points. If you followed the *triage* method, you earn 2 more points. And if you reviewed the test, a final 2 points are possible.

Use this record to keep up with how well you do on each test. By recording the solutions to testing errors, you will become a better student. By looking over the types of questions you missed, you can determine whether you are continuing to miss the same type of questions; if you are, you can practice and work on that particular type.

Keeping up with how you perform on tests allows you to improve as a test taker and as a student. It can be a major help in deciding what you need to emphasize for future study.

LEARNING FROM TESTS REVIEW QUESTIONS

1. Give three reasons why it is important to make each test a learning experience.

2. Explain the three major types of errors you can make on a test question.

3. Why is it important to arrive at a solution for correcting each error you make?

4. What can you learn from the Test-Taking Record when it has been used over time with several different tests?

LEARNING FROM TESTS EXERCISE

Make a copy of the Test-Taking Record and complete it for at least five tests. After the fifth test, consider how maintaining the record has improved your test-taking skills.

LEARNING FROM TESTS SUMMARY

A major purpose of taking a test is to learn from it. Understanding the mistakes you've made gives you valuable insights for future tests.

1. Right after the test, note what questions gave you trouble.

2. When you get the test back, correct all errors and learn the corrected answers.

3. Keep each test and use it for future reference.

4. Find out what you missed, why you missed it, and what sort of questions gave you trouble. Try to distinguish between the different types of error:

   a. *Type 1 error* – a careless mistake

   b. *Type 2 error* – lack of knowledge or skill

   c. *Type 3 error* – an incorrect choice

5. Use the Test-Taking Record.

CHAPTER 15

Papers and Written Reports

When writing, try to use the Preacher's Method we mentioned earlier: tell the readers what you're going to say, then tell them in detail, and then tell them what you told them.

THE WRITING PROCESS

Begin with as clear a statement of your thesis sentence as you can possibly manage. If you want to write about the ways in which George Washington was the father of his country, it's not a bad idea to begin with the statement, "George Washington was in many ways the father of his country." Avoid rambling introductions, such as "It was a dark and stormy day and George walked in out of the cherry orchard and his father hit him right between the eyes with a question." With your thesis statement in the first sentence, there can be no misunderstanding about what you're really trying to say.

The most important point to remember is that time is your best friend in essay writing. Try to begin as early as possible. The minute your instructor assigns a writing task, start thinking about what you want to write about. Keep it simple, and try to narrow it down; typically, students pick out a broader topic than they wind up writing on. Then, try to get an outline started. We include a "Preacher's Sandwich" model for preparing an outline (Figure 15-1) and a Five-Paragraph Paper Outline Form (Figure 15-2), either of which will help you organize and get started on an essay.

As soon as possible, write a draft, even if it's a shaggy dog of a draft. A working draft, no matter how shaggy, will give you something to edit, proofread, and expand. If possible, type the draft on a computer and run it through the spell-checker. Also get someone else to proof-read this draft; it is difficult for any writer to detect his or her own mistakes.

FIGURE 15-1.
The Preacher's Sandwich: Preparing to Write.

Topic

Title

Thesis Sentences:

      Subtopic A

      Subtopic B

      Subtopic C

Body

A

B

C

Conclusion

    1

    2

    3

Ending Sentence

FIGURE 15-2.
Five-Paragraph Paper: Outline Form

Copy this form (by hand or on a photocopier) and use it to plan out your papers. Don't worry about writing complete sentences on this form; just put down notes of the ideas you want to use. If you have the opportunity for a planning conference with your instructor or another advisor, fill in this form together before you begin writing your paper.

Bear in mind that not every paper has to follow this outline perfectly. You should use this as a guide, a helpful tool — don't feel restricted or limited by it. It is here to give you the skeleton of the paper, nothing more.

I. **Introduction**

    a) Introductory Sentence (Hook):

    _____

    b) Setting up the Topic (Motivator):

    _____

    c) Lead into the Thesis (Transition):

    _____

    d) Thesis Sentence (Main Idea):

    _____

II. **First Paragraph**

    a) Main Idea (Topic Sentence — supports thesis):

    _____

    b) First Example:

    _____

    c) Second Example:

    _____

    d) Third Example:

    _____

    e) Summary (Clincher):

    _____

III. Second Paragraph

a) Main Idea (Topic Sentence — supports thesis):

_____

b) First Example:

_____

c) Second Example:

_____

d) Third Example:

_____

e) Summary (Clincher):

_____

IV. Third Paragraph

a) Main Idea (Topic Sentence — supports thesis):

_____

b) First Example:

_____

c) Second Example:

_____

d) Third Example:

_____

e) Summary (Clincher):

_____

V. Conclusion

a) Restatement of Thesis:

_____

b) Summary:

_____

c) Evaluation (two sentences):

_____

d) Concluding Sentence:

_____

Make your next draft smoother and more professional. Get it edited and cleaned up; again, using other eyes than yours will be helpful. Four or five drafts are not too many to produce a really slick, professional paper. This is much easier to accomplish on a computer than in handwriting.

THE DIRTY DOZEN

Be sure to avoid what we call the Dirty Dozen, the 12 most common mistakes in student writing:

1. *Sloppiness or ugliness.* Make your paper look professional and attractive. With word processing, it's easy to turn in a beautiful paper. Most instructors tend to save their best grades for the best-looking papers.

2. *Illegible words and passages.* Clean up your handwriting, or fix your typewriter or computer, so that the instructor can read every word on your paper.

3. *Errors of form.* There are many essay forms to choose from, and students often follow the wrong ones. Find out what form your instructor wants you to follow — most instructors have preferences — and follow it very carefully.

4. *Errors in spelling.* There shouldn't be any spelling errors in the final draft. Use a spell-checker and a proofreader.

5. *Errors in grammar.* Find a proofreader with good grammar skills so there won't be any grammatical errors on your final draft. A grammar checker program for your computer may also be helpful as a first check.

6. *Errors in punctuation or capitalization.* Again, a good proofreader can help you avoid these costly mistakes.

7. *Sentence fragments.* Make sure your paper contains no leftover chunks of sentences. In academic writing, only complete sentences are acceptable.

8. *Run-on sentences.* Check your sentences to be sure none are run-ons. If a sentence is longer than 12 words, be suspicious.

9. *Errors of organization.* Write from an outline to avoid making errors of organization.

10. *Errors of logic.* If you're writing about something that you think is really wonderful or really terrible, watch yourself. Errors of logic tend to appear when the author is writing about topics very close to his or her heart; he or she is more likely to say things that can't

withstand a rigorous logical analysis by an unsympathetic instructor. Watch your logic, and check with your proofreader.

11. *Errors of fact.* Factual errors creep in everywhere, and are very difficult to avoid. We all think we know facts that we don't actually know. Check every fact, and make sure your proofreader does too.

12. *Overstatements.* Don't make extravagant claims. Think small. The less you claim on a certain point, the easier it is to defend. It is generally better to understate your points and conclusions. Tone down any extreme statements.

Those are the Dirty Dozen, and they are responsible for much mischief in students' writing. If you can avoid these, and you can get your papers in on time, you'll do well. Again, start early and make sure you meet the deadlines — or beat them by a little bit if possible. Instructors tend to grade papers kindly when they come in early, and those papers frequently get good grades. But certainly don't sacrifice the quality of your paper to get it in before the deadline.

CHAPTER 16

Oral Reports

Students are often asked to present oral reports to a class. Your grade on an oral report is a product of the quality of the material and the quality of your presentation. Like all of the other output functions, oral presentations involve performance, and performance demands preparation, practice, and acting out the appropriate skills. To give a good oral report, you need to start early, prepare thoroughly, practice the performance, and acquire the necessary skills for speaking in front of a group.

PREPARATION

In preparing for an oral report, it is extremely important to begin early. Beginning as soon as possible allows you to deal with the information over a long period of time. This mental incubation period gives your brain enough time to digest and organize the material effectively.

The first step in preparation is selecting a topic. Try to select a very narrow topic; as we have already mentioned, many students select topics that are much too broad. A broad topic is very difficult to cover well, and often only allows you to present broad strokes of ideas. In contrast, a narrow topic allows for more complete coverage. This results in a stronger, more focused argument, and makes it possible for you to deal with interesting and exciting details that bring the presentation to life.

As you narrow down your topic, you must find the resources to develop your presentation. Compile a bibliography of references that you will use in preparing the oral report. Organize the references with the author's last name first, then list them in alphabetical order and number them. This way, as you prepare your presentation, you can cite a given reference by number, instead of having to use the name of the author, the name of the book, and all the other citation material.

After you have selected your topic, identified your references, and developed your bibliography, you can begin gathering information for the report. It is wise to separate each piece of information from the others; you can do this by skipping a space after each idea. After all the information is gathered, cut each idea from the paper, so you have many small slips of paper with a separate idea on each slip. It is then possible to organize the ideas to form the entire presentation. If all the ideas from each reference were kept together, it would be nearly impossible to integrate the ideas to create a meaningful whole. Remember that when you organize a report, you are organizing ideas, not entire references. When each of your ideas is on a separate piece of paper, you can easily arrange and rearrange them.

The next step in developing a report is creating an outline of sentences or key words. The outline serves as the organizational structure for your ideas and as a guide for making the oral presentation. Frequently students transfer the outline from regular 8½ x 11" paper onto 3 x 5" index cards. Index cards are much less distracting to the viewer when the presentation is delivered. They also make it easier to practice the presentation while you are away from your place of study.

Since an oral report is not *read,* but *presented,* it is not necessary to write it out. (Of course, if the instructor requires you to also turn in a written report, you should write one.) One problem with writing out oral reports is that students typically read them word for word. It is better to stop at the outline stage and improvise a bit for your actual presentation. This keeps your presentation lively and your audience interested.

PRACTICE

Practice is the key to making a good presentation. One method of practice is to watch yourself deliver the report before a mirror. This allows you to see how the presentation is being made, and provides you with immediate feedback. As you look in the mirror, you can see yourself as others will see you; you can critique your presentation thoroughly and objectively, as if you were watching another person present. For the same reason, you should also record the practice on a tape recorder. On tape, your voice sounds very different from the way it normally sounds to you. It usually sounds like someone else (you may think it sounds horrible), and it allows you to make a more objective evaluation.

The tape recorder also has a much more important purpose. When you practice on tape, you can turn the tape recorder off to make changes in the presentation, to answer the phone, or to deal with any other interruptions. This allows the practice to be accurately timed. You can then adjust the length of the presentation to the instructor's time requirements. Videotape can be even better than audio, although the TV camera is harder to ignore. Videotaping brings out the ham in the best of us, but it is a fine editing tool.

Just like any other academic work, an oral report needs to be edited carefully. Practice your oral report in front of a friend, and encourage him or her to be critical. Your friend can tell you if the report makes sense, if it is boring, or if any aspects of the presentation should be improved. The best reports have been thoroughly critiqued by someone other than the presenter.

Refine and practice your report until you can't wait to give it. You know you are ready when you want to be the first to present your report. If you have practiced until you really want to deliver the report, the entire presentation takes on a different quality. Your performance improves sharply, and stage fright is greatly diminished. Stage fright is much like test anxiety; when your mind is on the presentation rather than on the consequences of making a fool of yourself, stage fright is under control.

Wanting to perform also makes your movements more natural. When you make a public presentation, worrying about your hands can be a severe problem; you may wonder whether you should hold your hands behind your back, to the side, or folded in front of your body. If you really want to tell the oral report, however, your hands become a part of the presentation. Gestures become natural, automatic. Your entire body gets involved in the presentation, and you suddenly find that your hands take care of themselves.

PRESENTATION

When you give an oral report, you should dress well and look your best. The way you look greatly affects the way you view yourself, and the way you feel about yourself when making a presentation will affect the outcome. Try to look good, but do not overdress. A general guideline is that your clothes should not distract listeners from what you have to say or from the overall effect of the report. As a rule, dress a little bit better than you ordinarily would for the class.

When the time comes to make your presentation, begin by getting the attention of the group. Very often, your listeners will have little or no interest in the topic of the report. It is your responsibility to get them interested. One way to attract interest is to tell a joke. Keep in mind that the joke should be on the subject, and that telling a joke in front of a captive group is very different from telling a joke to your friends. If no one laughs, your presentation will get off to a bad start that is very difficult to overcome. However, if the joke is funny and on the subject, and you can make it funny before a group, it can be very effective in gaining interest.

Another way to gain attention is to begin with an interesting quotation. Quotations that are controversial, that signify danger, or that cause an emotional response will gain attention. Again, the quotation should relate to the subject of the oral presentation. It should be in good taste and not offend any members of the group. A relevant, appropriate quote from the Bible or other religious book will usually gain attention; our culture has instilled into people the feeling that they must pay attention when a religious text is read.

You may also gain the group's attention with a rhetorical question, a question that gets people thinking but that no one is expected to answer, such as, "What is the Truth?" Ask a question that somehow relates to the people in the group. The question should get the group to begin following your train of thought. Once the group is thinking about what you are saying, you have gained the attention necessary to continue with the presentation.

Another way to gain attention is to use silence. Stand looking at the group for 10 seconds, without saying anything. The members of the group will start thinking that you have forgotten what to say, and they will begin to pull for you. If you are able to say nothing for as long as 15 seconds, your classmates will be on the edge of their seats, anxiously waiting for anything to break the silence. This ploy takes great courage, and you need to tell the instructor about the method before you begin the presentation. Otherwise, the instructor may interfere, because silence is just as disturbing for an instructor as it is for a group.

After gaining the attention of the class, use the Preacher's Method of communication:

- First, *tell them what you are going to tell them.* Provide a clear and succinct introduction to the oral presentation. Cover all the major points that you will make in the presentation.

- Second, *tell them.* At this point you should give the entire presentation with all the details.

- Finally, *tell them what you told them.* A good summary of the presentation with an appropriate closing is the final element of the oral report.

While gaining attention is important, keeping attention during the details of the presentation is equally crucial. A presentation that will earn a good grade is not boring. It is easier to hold your listeners' attention when you truly want to tell the story. Your enthusiasm will be catching, and enthusiasm maintains attention. Another method for keeping listeners' attention is to modulate your voice throughout the presentation. A monotone will drive listeners away. Your voice and speech pattern should vary in tone, in speed, in loudness, and in intensity; no single speech pattern is appropriate for all parts of a report. One speech variation you can use is a stage whisper. This is a very effective attention holder; a listener is required to pay more attention to a whisper than to a shout.

For your speech to be successful, you must also have an impressive closing. The first thing you say and the last thing you say are the two ideas most often recalled. A memorable closing, coupled with an attention-getting introduction, will create bookends to the presentation that help produce an excellent report. If you begin the presentation with a joke, it is valuable to end with a joke. Likewise, if you begin with a quotation or with a rhetorical question, using the same technique at the closing often works well. (Of course, if the presentation begins with silence, you cannot end the report with silence. Some other closing must be employed.)

CHAPTER 17

Class Participation as Output

Most grades take into account test scores, written assignments, and possibly oral presentations, which may be used in varying combinations. In addition, some measure of class participation is factored into grades by almost all instructors, either consciously or unconsciously. It is difficult for an instructor to ignore how a student participated in class when he or she begins to determine the student's grade. Class participation as output is much more than being involved in class discussion. It is important that you show up on time, ready for class, and looking like you want to be there. Attend class whenever you are physically able to get there. Class participation also includes listening, note taking, posture and body language in the classroom, eye contact with the instructor, and completion of required work ahead of time.

LISTENING

Usually instructors are keenly aware of the students who listen actively and are attuned to the overall class action. They are equally aware of those students who are in class physically, but not mentally. Listening is not only a method for obtaining the information needed to perform well; it is also a way to show that you are interested in the instructor's lesson and in the subject itself. Most instructors have a great interest in the material they teach. A student who shows genuine interest in what the instructor finds interesting will generally be thought of as a good student by that instructor.

NOTE TAKING

Instructors are also aware of students who take notes. Instructors are usually good students themselves, and they understand that listening and note taking are the main components of effective study. When an instructor observes a student diligently taking notes on a regular basis, he or she recognizes that student as one who intends to do well. Again, the student has planted a seed in the instructor's mind that "this is a good student."

BODY LANGUAGE

In the classroom, body language speaks louder than words. Body language communicates your attitude, your interest, and your intention better than any verbal expression. A student who comes in late, slouches, looks bored or gazes out the window, and appears to have no interest in the subject, is viewed by most instructors as a poor student. In contrast, when you arrive on time, show interest, lean toward the instructor, have paper and pencils ready for note taking, sit upright in your desk, and maintain eye contact with the instructor, you are seen as a good student. No amount of telling the instructor that the class was great will compensate for poor body language. Instructors would much rather see students perform successfully in class than hear all types of compliments after class. It is nearly impossible to make an instructor think you enjoyed a class when your poor body language belies your statement.

EYE CONTACT

Good students maintain eye contact with the instructor. Appropriate eye contact is one of the best types of positive communication one person can make with another. This is especially true in the classroom. Instructors teach to the students who maintain eye contact. In some sense, your eyes give you away. Instructors can often tell what is going on in your mind by the look of your eyes. If a student's eyes have a blank expression, the student does not appear to be engaged in class. If a student's eyes show interest, understanding, and appreciation, that student is viewed as intelligent and involved. Make sure the instructor sees your eyes as the class progresses. When the instructor sees your eyes light up, it is clear that you understand the material. Your eyes light up only when you catch on or learn; this cannot be faked.

The instructor's job is to help students to learn, to foster understanding. Your job as a student is to learn and to understand. When instructors see your eyes light up, they know they have done a good job — and few experiences feel better than doing a good job. Your instructors will feel good about themselves and about you.

COMPLETING ASSIGNMENTS EARLY

Good students also complete their assignments before they are due. Few acts impress an instructor more than turning work in early. Instructors must grade all assigned work, and the press of time for grading usually occurs toward due dates. Students who delay and get assignments in at the last possible moment force the instructor to rush. Students who complete assignments early appear to be better students, and are likely to get better grades.

ESTABLISHING YOURSELF AS A GOOD STUDENT

Why should you care what an instructor thinks about you? Generally, instructors do not let "good students" get poor grades. Instructors expect those they view as good students to perform well. If a "good student" does not perform well, the instructor will wonder what caused this poor performance, why the expectations he or she had for that student have not been met. At that point, it is not unusual for the instructor to check to see if the student was ill or if some other factor caused this unexpected event. The situation is quite different if the instructor believes an individual is a poor student, or has no feeling one way or another about the student; if that student performs poorly, the instructor has no reason to wonder why. Class participation, good or bad, establishes the instructor's mind-set about a student. Instructors notice elements of class participation far more than most students realize.

CLASS PARTICIPATION REVIEW QUESTIONS

1. Why is the intention to participate the first step toward good class involvement?

2. What do you feel is the most important attitude for you, if you are to get the most from a class?

3. Do you feel you are an aggressive class participant? If not, what do you think you have to do to become one?

4. Do you usually prepare before you go to class? Do you see why prior preparation is important?

5. Name three ways mentioned in the text for you to prepare to go to class.

6. Can you name other ways to prepare prior to attending class?

7. Name the major input skills for effective study.

CLASS PARTICIPATION EXERCISES

1. Team up with another student and carry out the following steps:

   a. Prepare for class, with one of you using the preview technique and the other using the questioning approach.

   b. Do what is necessary to prepare for note taking.

   c. Discuss the attitudes you need for good class participation. Add other attitudes that you think will support your effectiveness.

   d. Attend the class, take notes, and participate as expected.

   e. After class, discuss with each other how that class was different from other classes. Go over both sets of notes and note any improvements.

2. List ten or more reasons why appropriate class participation is helpful in obtaining good grades.

3. Discuss with your friends how you can improve your class participation skills.

CARDINAL RULES FOR OUTPUT

1. Overlearn the details. Tests are on details.

2. Follow the *triage* method. Answer the questions you know for sure; possibles and long shots rob you of time on tests.

3. Have a test schedule that is related to the value of each question.

4. Your objective when taking a test is to prove what you know.

5. Try to prove true/false statements false.

6. Read all the answers on multiple-choice tests before you respond.

7. Good-luck charms work on tests. Carry some with you.

8. Avoid test anxiety. Be in control of what you think.

9. Keep a record of every test you take. Know why you missed what you missed, and find a way to correct your errors.

10. Avoid the Dirty Dozen when writing papers.

11. Start papers *early.*

12. Get someone else to edit every paper you write.

13. Practice an oral report until you can't wait to tell it.

14. Every grade includes class participation.

15. Keep your eyes on the instructor's eyes.

CONCLUSION

A Formula for Success

In this book, we have outlined a systematic approach to studying that was begun at Harvard and extended and revised into a system at Venture School, Ben Franklin Academy, Emory University, and Study Skills Associates. We have worked hard to bring about a system of studying that can help any student to learn more, get better grades, and get more satisfaction out of school.

Your task in school is to gain knowledge and understanding. Earlier in our discussion we drew a distinction between these two terms. Most students gain understanding; they have a fairly clear picture of the material they study, but do not necessarily have detailed knowledge of definitions, terms, formulas, minor characters, and so on. Unfortunately, many tests focus on details, and students are usually graded on detailed knowledge. In order to learn effectively and get good grades, you need to understand overall ideas, but you also need to memorize the supporting details.

Following the strategies outlined in this book will help you to develop both general understanding and detailed knowledge. We have shown you how to study in a timely and effective way, how to maximize your learning in class and through your reading. We have also shown you how to maximize your performance on tests, papers, and oral reports. We have indicated ways you can set realistic goals and check on your progress toward those goals. All of these are ways of becoming a better student in attitude, design, and performance. As you improve each part of your learning and study system, all the other parts will improve as well. We repeatedly find that students who learn to apply all these skills become much more productive and successful.

In any endeavor, three important elements — high expectations for yourself, hustle, and competence in your area of performance — are essential to performing well. In academic settings, high expectations, hustle, and study skills will produce success.

EXPECTATIONS

You are limited by your own expectations of yourself. Keep in mind three principles concerning thoughts and their effects on performance:

1. The potential of the human being is far greater in extent and diversity than you have ever imagined.

2. A great portion of significant human experience is comprised of unconscious processes.

3. The most important of these unconscious processes are our own expectations, our images of ourselves, the limitations we place on ourselves, and our images of the future. All of these limit or enhance our capabilities.

Do you feel you are performing to your potential? In all likelihood, you know you are not even coming close to performing what you are capable of performing; few people do. Begin taking steps to approach your potential. Learn to use more and more of your ability.

First, try to think more highly of yourself. What you think about yourself always has an effect on your unconscious thoughts. Your unconscious thoughts are products of all your experiences and what other people have told you about you. People may have told you again and again how poorly you are doing, how much you need to improve, or how unimportant you are. Never take a single comment or source as the measure of what and who you are. You can overcome unconscious negativity by consciously thinking positively. Every day, take a moment or two to think of doing well, of how good you are, and of achieving excellence. You become what you think about yourself.

Think about the limits you place on yourself. Since no one can do all things, you are forced to limit yourself to some degree. You will generally choose to do the things you find easiest and most enjoyable for you. As you develop priorities, keep in mind that your priorities represent what you *want* to do, not all you *can* do. You have chosen. You were not forced. Your limitations are few, and your potential is boundless.

Your vision of your future is also extremely important. You are limited by that vision. You are unable to achieve, perform, or become more than the vision you hold for yourself. Do you see yourself as being confident, successful, and fulfilled? Enhance your vision of yourself and you will enhance who and what you are and will be.

HUSTLE

Success is affected not only by your expectations for yourself, but also by what you do about others' expectations for you. You are in an interesting situation. You cannot achieve beyond your own expectations for yourself, but you must perform beyond the expectations of others. Exceeding the expectations placed on you involves *hustle*. When you hustle, you do more than is asked of you, and you complete your work early.

One executive illustrated the value of hustle with the following anecdote. He had asked a person to perform a task and was told by that individual, "That is not in my job description." The executive responded, "You are right. Please continue what you are doing." The manager then asked another person with the same job to perform that task. This worker said, "Wow! Thanks for the opportunity." The executive asks each of us, "Who do you think will get a raise or be promoted — the person who limited themselves to the job they have now, or the one who was willing to go beyond it?"

You must hustle all your life if you expect to succeed. The successful business is the one that provides a greater service or product than you expect, that gives you more than you pay for. Likewise, the successful student does more than the instructor asks and completes work before it is due.

STUDY SKILLS

To be a successful student, you also need appropriate study skills. Success requires competence. Successful students possess the input skills of listening, note taking, reading, and class participation; the process skills of memory, concentration, daily review, self and time management, and class participation; and the output skills of test taking, writing, oral presentations, and class participation.

THE FORMULA FOR SUCCESS

The formula for success can be expressed as follows:

$$S = H(IS + PS + OS + SE)$$

S = academic SUCCESS

H = HUSTLE

IS = INPUT skills

PS = PROCESS skills

OS = OUTPUT skills

SE = high SELF EXPECTATIONS

Your skills and your self expectations are summative; each adds to your success. Hustle is the key contributor to your success because it multiplies the effectiveness of all the other factors.

Go to class with the intent to listen actively and take good notes. Outside class, read the material, review your notes daily, use study cards for details, concentrate well, use your memory and recall tools, and manage your time and yourself. To show what you have learned, use your test-taking skills, write good papers and oral reports, and participate fully in class. If you follow these guidelines, your expectations for good grades will increase, and the expectations of others for you will increase. But remember that hustle is the multiplying factor. Add hustle to this equation, and you will truly be an exceptional student.

Cardinal Rules
for Study Power

1. Listening is the primary study skill.

2. You recall what you see or hear often over time.

3. A little study every day is superior to a great deal of it in one day.

4. An accurate, reliable set of notes is the foundation of good study.

5. Summarize briefly in your own words.

6. Read with successive approximations.

7. Know something about what you are going to read before you read it.

8. Designate each idea separately when taking notes.

9. Review your notes every day for at least 5 days.

10. Use study cards to learn details.

11. Keep a daily and weekly calendar. Try not to have too much to do in any one week or on any one day.

12. A practice test is excellent test preparation.

13. Remember the *triage.*

14. Your brain works best when it is given adequate time. Give it time by beginning early.

15. Go to class with a fairly good idea of what will happen there.

16. Learning favors the prepared mind.

17. Intention is the first step to excellence.

18. Spend some time every day on each course you are taking.

19. HUSTLE!

INDEX

outlines
    as study tools 80, 94, 99
    of lecture content 11, 17, 28, 47
    of reports 55, 57–96, 59, 68, 69, 118, 120,
        121, 122, 125
output skills 3, 6–8, 9, 101–133, 136, 137
overlearning 100, 106, 110, 112, 133

P

paper
    law-ruled 18, 22, 25
    loose-leaf 18, 25, 45
partnerships
    for creating practice tests 96
    for learning from tests 113
    for listening 11, 13
    for note taking 21, 24, 25
persistence 8, 72
pictures
    as distractions 45, 72
    as organizational structures 80, 94, 99
    in study reading 27, 34, 35
    memorization of 86, 88
planning
    in decision making 41–42, 42, 50
    long-range 43 48, 49, 50
    of reports 120
    of test strategies 111, 116
    of time use 6, 46, 47, 51, 67, 71, 75
    short-range 43, 44, 50
    written 44, 111, 116, 120
possibles 103, 106, 133
practice
    for oral reports 58, 59, 64, 124–126, 133
    for tests 94–96, 97, 98, 100, 110, 112, 116
    in concentrating 71, 72
Preacher's Method 39
    of listening 11, 13, 16
    of reading 27 29, 33
    of speaking 127
    of writing 105, 118
prediction
    of lecture content 11, 12, 47
    of test questions 11, 12, 13, 16, 18, 18–38,
        25, 26, 32, 36, 47, 77, 96, 97

preparation
    for class participation 38, 76, 132
    for listening 11, 13, 16, 24, 28, 30, 47, 51, 63
    for note taking 24, 132
    for reading 35
    for tests 2, 5, 9, 17, 40, 92–96, 102, 106,
        110, 113, 138
    of reports 7, 55, 58, 59, 124–125
    to concentrate 71
previewing
    as preparation for class 11, 28, 47, 132
    in study reading 27, 28, 29, 30, 32, 33, 34, 35
    of reference materials 46
    of tests 102, 107, 116
prime study time 47, 51, 63, 70
probables 102, 106, 107
process skills 3, 5–8, 40–100, 136, 137
proofreading 119, 122, 123

Q

questions
    asked in class 5, 12, 13, 28, 38, 90
    asked in notes 22
    asked in study reading 28, 36
    asked in summarizing 30, 90
    asked on tests 27, 30, 35, 36
    rhetorical 127
    to form structures 93, 98, 99, 107
    who, what, when, where, why, and how 16,
        19, 25, 30, 33, 34, 38, 90

R

reading
    active 27, 28, 33, 35, 36
    concentration and 70
    for pleasure 32, 33, 34
    importance of 9
    of resource material 57
    speed of 2, 32, 33, 39
    vs. studying 33, 39
recall
    anxiety and 109
    daily review and 5
    definition of 83
    enhancement of 5, 18, 21, 22, 83–90

ABOUT THE AUTHORS

William R. "Ron" Luckie has taught study skills for over 20 years. He operated a private middle school designed to help students who were not succeeding in other schooling situations. He served as the Director of Planning, Research and Evaluation for the Georgia State Board of Education. He has been a teacher, counselor, school principal, and college instructor; his experience in teaching and schooling spans over 40 years. Dr. Luckie is presently the director of Study Skills Associates — an organization involved in providing study skill workshops for schools, colleges, businesses, and government agencies; researching improved study practices; providing individual study support to students in an effort to identify and test improved study techniques; and supporting parents in helping their children in school.

Wood Smethurst is the co-founder and headmaster of the innovative Ben Franklin Academy in Atlanta, Georgia. He was also one of the founders of Atlanta's other innovative schools, Paideia and the Galloway School. He was previously the director of Emory University's Reading Center and Catch-Up School. He is the author of *Teaching Young Children to Read* and the forthcoming *Helping Your Child Become a Good Reader,* as well as numerous professional articles. He has taught for 37 years in public and private schools and universities.

THE STUDY POWER WORKBOOK

Mail this form with your payment to: BROOKLINE BOOKS
P.O. Box 1047
Cambridge, MA 02238-1047

If the form is missing—or to place any credit card order or request a catalog—please call (617) 868-0360 or 1-800-666-BOOK.

YES! Increase my Study Power even more!

Send me the *Study Power Workbook* (available in 1998).

Number of copies: _____ x **$12.95** = $ _____

MA residents add 5% sales tax = $ _____

Shipping and handling: **$1.50** per copy = $ _____

Total = $ _____

Name _____

Address _____

City, State, ZIP _____

Phone _____

E-mail _____

❏ Check enclosed (in U.S. funds, payable to Brookline Books).

❏ Please bill my: ❏ Visa ❏ MasterCard ❏ American Express

Card No. _____

Signature _____

❏ Please send me a catalog of Brookline Books titles.

BROOKLINE BOOKS Attn: Order Dept. • P.O. Box 1047 • Cambridge, MA 02238-1047